My Vintage Trailer RV Travel & Camping Journal

_____

"Traveling leaves you speechless, then turns you into a storyteller."

- Ibn Battuta

Copyright © 2017 Vintage Pen Press

All rights reserved. No part of this publication may be resold, hired out, transmitted or reproduced in any form by any electronic or mechanical means including photocopying, recording, or information storage and retrieval without prior written authority from the publishers.

ISBN-13: 978-1975864040
ISBN-10: 1975864042

VINTAGE PEN PRESS
Visit Us
www.vintagepenpress.com

Date: _____

From: _____

To: _____

Route Taken: _____

_____

Weather:

Beginning Mileage: _____

Ending Mileage: _____

Total Miles Traveled: _____

Campground Information

Name: _____

Address: _____

Phone: _____

Site # _____ $ _____ ☐ Day ☐ Week ☐ Month

☐ First Visit ☐ Return Visit ☐ Easy Access
☐ Site Level ☐ Back-in ☐ Pull-through
☐ 15 amp ☐ 30 amp ☐ 50 amp
☐ Water ☐ Sewer ☐ Shade ☐ Sun
☐ Paved ☐ Sand / Grass ☐ Gravel
☐ Picnic Table ☐ Fire ring ☐ Trees ☐ Lawn
☐ Patio ☐ Kid Friendly ☐ Pet Friendly
☐ Store ☐ Cafe ☐ Firewood
☐ Ice ☐ Secuiryt ☐ Quiet ☐ Noisy

Our Rating: ☆ ☆ ☆ ☆ ☆

GPS: _____

Altitude: _____

Cell Service / Carrier: _____

☐ Antenna Reception ☐ Satellite TV ☐ Cable TV
☐ Wifi Available ☐ Free ☐ Fee $_____

Memberships: _____

Ammenities: _____

Location	☺	😐	☹	Water Pressure	☺	😐	☹
Restrooms	☺	😐	☹	Laundry	☺	😐	☹
Pool	☺	😐	☹	Hot Tub	☺	😐	☹

PLACES VISITED / ACTIVITIES: _____

_____

_____

_____

PEOPLE MET / NEW FRIENDS: _____

_____

_____

_____

FOOD, DINING & RESTAURANTS: _____

_____

_____

_____

HIGHLIGHTS / MEMORABLE EVENTS: _____

_____

_____

_____

PLACES TO GO & THINGS TO DO FOR NEXT TIME: _____

_____

_____

_____

Notes:

Date: _____

Weather:

From: _____
To: _____
Route Taken: _____
_____

Beginning Mileage: _____

Ending Mileage: _____

Total Miles Traveled: _____

CAMPGROUND INFORMATION

Name: _____
Address: _____
Phone: _____

Site # _____ $ _____ ☐ Day ☐ Week ☐ Month

☐ First Visit   ☐ Return Visit   ☐ Easy Access
☐ Site Level   ☐ Back-in   ☐ Pull-through
☐ 15 amp   ☐ 30 amp   ☐ 50 amp
☐ Water   ☐ Sewer   ☐ Shade   ☐ Sun
☐ Paved   ☐ Sand / Grass   ☐ Gravel
☐ Picnic Table   ☐ Fire ring   ☐ Trees   ☐ Lawn
☐ Patio   ☐ Kid Friendly   ☐ Pet Friendly
☐ Store   ☐ Cafe   ☐ Firewood
☐ Ice   ☐ Secuiryt   ☐ Quiet   ☐ Noisy

Our Rating: ☆ ☆ ☆ ☆ ☆
GPS: _____
Altitude: _____
Cell Service / Carrier: _____
☐ Antenna Reception   ☐ Satellite TV   ☐ Cable TV
☐ Wifi Available   ☐ Free ☐ Fee $_____
Memberships: _____
Ammenities: _____

Location   ☺ ☻ ☹   Water Pressure ☺ ☻ ☹
Restrooms   ☺ ☻ ☹   Laundry   ☺ ☻ ☹
Pool   ☺ ☻ ☹   Hot Tub   ☺ ☻ ☹

PLACES VISITED / ACTIVITIES: _____
_____
_____
_____

PEOPLE MET / NEW FRIENDS: _____
_____
_____
_____

FOOD, DINING & RESTAURANTS: _____
_____
_____
_____

HIGHLIGHTS / MEMORABLE EVENTS: _____
_____
_____
_____

PLACES TO GO & THINGS TO DO FOR NEXT TIME: _____
_____
_____
_____

Notes:

Date: _____
Weather:

From: _____
To: _____
Route Taken: _____
_____

Beginning Mileage: _____
Ending Mileage: _____
Total Miles Traveled: _____

Campground Information

Name: _____
Address: _____
Phone: _____

Site # _____ $ _____ ☐ Day ☐ Week ☐ Month
☐ First Visit   ☐ Return Visit   ☐ Easy Access
☐ Site Level   ☐ Back-in   ☐ Pull-through
☐ 15 amp   ☐ 30 amp   ☐ 50 amp
☐ Water   ☐ Sewer   ☐ Shade   ☐ Sun
☐ Paved   ☐ Sand / Grass   ☐ Gravel
☐ Picnic Table   ☐ Fire ring   ☐ Trees   ☐ Lawn
☐ Patio   ☐ Kid Friendly   ☐ Pet Friendly
☐ Store   ☐ Cafe   ☐ Firewood
☐ Ice   ☐ Secuiryt   ☐ Quiet   ☐ Noisy

Our Rating: ☆ ☆ ☆ ☆ ☆
GPS: _____
Altitude: _____
Cell Service / Carrier: _____
☐ Antenna Reception   ☐ Satellite TV   ☐ Cable TV
☐ Wifi Available   ☐ Free ☐ Fee $_____
Memberships: _____
Ammenities: _____

Location	☺	😐	☹	Water Pressure	☺	😐	☹
Restrooms	☺	😐	☹	Laundry	☺	😐	☹
Pool	☺	😐	☹	Hot Tub	☺	😐	☹

Places Visited / Activities:
_____
_____
_____
_____

People Met / New Friends:
_____
_____
_____
_____

Food, Dining & Restaurants:
_____
_____
_____
_____

Highlights / Memorable Events:
_____
_____
_____
_____

Places To Go & Things To Do for Next Time:
_____
_____
_____
_____

NOTES:

Date: _____

Weather:

From: _____
To: _____
Route Taken: _____
_____

Beginning Mileage: _____

Ending Mileage: _____

Total Miles Traveled: _____

CAMPGROUND INFORMATION

Name: _____
Address: _____
Phone: _____

Site # _____ $ _____

- [ ] First Visit
- [ ] Site Level
- [ ] 15 amp
- [ ] Water
- [ ] Paved
- [ ] Picnic Table
- [ ] Patio
- [ ] Store
- [ ] Ice

- [ ] Return Visit
- [ ] Back-in
- [ ] 30 amp
- [ ] Sewer
- [ ] Sand / Grass
- [ ] Fire ring
- [ ] Kid Friendly
- [ ] Cafe
- [ ] Secuiryt

- [ ] Day - [ ] Week - [ ] Month
- [ ] Easy Access
- [ ] Pull-through
- [ ] 50 amp
- [ ] Shade   - [ ] Sun
- [ ] Gravel
- [ ] Trees   - [ ] Lawn
- [ ] Pet Friendly
- [ ] Firewood
- [ ] Quiet   - [ ] Noisy

Our Rating: ☆ ☆ ☆ ☆ ☆

GPS: _____
Altitude: _____
Cell Service / Carrier: _____

- [ ] Antenna Reception   - [ ] Satellite TV   - [ ] Cable TV
- [ ] Wifi Available   - [ ] Free - [ ] Fee $_____

Memberships: _____
Ammenities: _____

	😊 😐 ☹		😊 😐 ☹
Location		Water Pressure	
Restrooms		Laundry	
Pool		Hot Tub	

PLACES VISITED / ACTIVITIES: _____
_____
_____
_____

PEOPLE MET / NEW FRIENDS: _____
_____
_____
_____

FOOD, DINING & RESTAURANTS: _____
_____
_____
_____

HIGHLIGHTS / MEMORABLE EVENTS: _____
_____
_____
_____

PLACES TO GO & THINGS TO DO FOR NEXT TIME: _____
_____
_____
_____

Notes:

Date: _____

Weather:

From: _____
To: _____
Route Taken: _____
_____

Beginning Mileage: _____

Ending Mileage: _____

Total Miles Traveled: _____

Campground Information

Name: _____
Address: _____
Phone: _____

Site #_____ $_____ ☐ Day ☐ Week ☐ Month

☐ First Visit   ☐ Return Visit   ☐ Easy Access
☐ Site Level   ☐ Back-in   ☐ Pull-through
☐ 15 amp   ☐ 30 amp   ☐ 50 amp
☐ Water   ☐ Sewer   ☐ Shade   ☐ Sun
☐ Paved   ☐ Sand / Grass   ☐ Gravel
☐ Picnic Table   ☐ Fire ring   ☐ Trees   ☐ Lawn
☐ Patio   ☐ Kid Friendly   ☐ Pet Friendly
☐ Store   ☐ Cafe   ☐ Firewood
☐ Ice   ☐ Secuiryt   ☐ Quiet   ☐ Noisy

Our Rating: ☆ ☆ ☆ ☆ ☆
GPS: _____
Altitude: _____
Cell Service / Carrier: _____
☐ Antenna Reception   ☐ Satellite TV   ☐ Cable TV
☐ Wifi Available   ☐ Free ☐ Fee $_____
Memberships: _____
Ammenities: _____

Location	☺ ☺ ☹	Water Pressure	☺ ☺ ☹
Restrooms	☺ ☺ ☹	Laundry	☺ ☺ ☹
Pool	☺ ☺ ☹	Hot Tub	☺ ☺ ☹

Places Visited / Activities: _____
_____
_____
_____

People Met / New Friends: _____
_____
_____
_____

Food, Dining & Restaurants: _____
_____
_____
_____

Highlights / Memorable Events: _____
_____
_____
_____

Places To Go & Things To Do for Next Time: _____
_____
_____
_____

Notes:

Date: _____   From: _____   Beginning Mileage: _____

Weather: To: _____   Ending Mileage: _____

                         Route Taken: _____
                         _____   Total Miles Traveled: _____

Campground Information

Name: _____

Address: _____

Phone: _____

Site # _____ $ _____ ☐ Day ☐ Week ☐ Month

☐ First Visit   ☐ Return Visit   ☐ Easy Access
☐ Site Level   ☐ Back-in   ☐ Pull-through
☐ 15 amp   ☐ 30 amp   ☐ 50 amp
☐ Water   ☐ Sewer   ☐ Shade   ☐ Sun
☐ Paved   ☐ Sand / Grass   ☐ Gravel
☐ Picnic Table   ☐ Fire ring   ☐ Trees   ☐ Lawn
☐ Patio   ☐ Kid Friendly   ☐ Pet Friendly
☐ Store   ☐ Cafe   ☐ Firewood
☐ Ice   ☐ Secuiryt   ☐ Quiet   ☐ Noisy

Our Rating: ☆ ☆ ☆ ☆ ☆

GPS: _____

Altitude: _____

Cell Service / Carrier: _____

☐ Antenna Reception   ☐ Satellite TV   ☐ Cable TV
☐ Wifi Available   ☐ Free ☐ Fee $_____

Memberships: _____

Ammenities: _____

Location   ☺ ☹ ☹   Water Pressure ☺ ☹ ☹
Restrooms ☺ ☹ ☹   Laundry   ☺ ☹ ☹
Pool   ☺ ☹ ☹   Hot Tub   ☺ ☹ ☹

Places Visited / Activities: _____

_____

_____

_____

People Met / New Friends: _____

_____

_____

_____

Food, Dining & Restaurants: _____

_____

_____

_____

Highlights / Memorable Events: _____

_____

_____

_____

Places To Go & Things To Do for Next Time: _____

_____

_____

_____

NOTES:

Date: _____
Weather:

From: _____
To: _____
Route Taken: _____
_____

Beginning Mileage: _____
Ending Mileage: _____
Total Miles Traveled: _____

Campground Information

Name: _____
Address: _____
Phone: _____

Site # _____ $ _____ ☐ Day ☐ Week ☐ Month

- ☐ First Visit
- ☐ Site Level
- ☐ 15 amp
- ☐ Water
- ☐ Paved
- ☐ Picnic Table
- ☐ Patio
- ☐ Store
- ☐ Ice

- ☐ Return Visit
- ☐ Back-in
- ☐ 30 amp
- ☐ Sewer
- ☐ Sand / Grass
- ☐ Fire ring
- ☐ Kid Friendly
- ☐ Cafe
- ☐ Secuiryt

- ☐ Easy Access
- ☐ Pull-through
- ☐ 50 amp
- ☐ Shade   ☐ Sun
- ☐ Gravel
- ☐ Trees   ☐ Lawn
- ☐ Pet Friendly
- ☐ Firewood
- ☐ Quiet   ☐ Noisy

Our Rating: ☆ ☆ ☆ ☆ ☆
GPS: _____
Altitude: _____
Cell Service / Carrier: _____

- ☐ Antenna Reception
- ☐ Wifi Available

☐ Satellite TV   ☐ Cable TV
☐ Free   ☐ Fee $ _____

Memberships: _____
Ammenities: _____

	☺ ☺ ☹		☺ ☺ ☹
Location		Water Pressure	
Restrooms		Laundry	
Pool		Hot Tub	

Places Visited / Activities: _____
_____
_____
_____

People Met / New Friends: _____
_____
_____
_____

Food, Dining & Restaurants: _____
_____
_____
_____

Highlights / Memorable Events: _____
_____
_____
_____

Places To Go & Things To Do for Next Time: _____
_____
_____
_____

Notes:

Date: _____

Weather:

From: _____

To: _____

Route Taken: _____

_____

Beginning Mileage: _____

Ending Mileage: _____

Total Miles Traveled: _____

Campground Information

Name: _____

Address: _____

Phone: _____

Site # _____ $ _____ ☐ Day ☐ Week ☐ Month

☐ First Visit   ☐ Return Visit   ☐ Easy Access
☐ Site Level   ☐ Back-in   ☐ Pull-through
☐ 15 amp   ☐ 30 amp   ☐ 50 amp
☐ Water   ☐ Sewer   ☐ Shade   ☐ Sun
☐ Paved   ☐ Sand / Grass   ☐ Gravel
☐ Picnic Table   ☐ Fire ring   ☐ Trees   ☐ Lawn
☐ Patio   ☐ Kid Friendly   ☐ Pet Friendly
☐ Store   ☐ Cafe   ☐ Firewood
☐ Ice   ☐ Secuiryt   ☐ Quiet   ☐ Noisy

Our Rating: ☆ ☆ ☆ ☆ ☆

GPS: _____

Altitude: _____

Cell Service / Carrier: _____

☐ Antenna Reception   ☐ Satellite TV   ☐ Cable TV
☐ Wifi Available   ☐ Free ☐ Fee $_____

Memberships: _____

Ammenities: _____

Location	☺	😐	☹	Water Pressure	☺	😐	☹
Restrooms	☺	😐	☹	Laundry	☺	😐	☹
Pool	☺	😐	☹	Hot Tub	☺	😐	☹

Places Visited / Activities: _____

_____

_____

_____

People Met / New Friends: _____

_____

_____

_____

Food, Dining & Restaurants: _____

_____

_____

_____

Highlights / Memorable Events: _____

_____

_____

_____

Places To Go & Things To Do for Next Time: _____

_____

_____

_____

Notes:

Date: _____

Weather:

From: _____
To: _____
Route Taken: _____
_____

Beginning Mileage: _____

Ending Mileage: _____

Total Miles Traveled: _____

CAMPGROUND INFORMATION

Our Rating: ☆ ☆ ☆ ☆ ☆

Name: _____
Address: _____
Phone: _____

GPS: _____
Altitude: _____

Site # _____ $ _____ ☐ Day ☐ Week ☐ Month
- ☐ First Visit
- ☐ Site Level
- ☐ 15 amp
- ☐ Water
- ☐ Paved
- ☐ Picnic Table
- ☐ Patio
- ☐ Store
- ☐ Ice

- ☐ Return Visit
- ☐ Back-in
- ☐ 30 amp
- ☐ Sewer
- ☐ Sand / Grass
- ☐ Fire ring
- ☐ Kid Friendly
- ☐ Cafe
- ☐ Secuiryt

- ☐ Easy Access
- ☐ Pull-through
- ☐ 50 amp
- ☐ Shade ☐ Sun
- ☐ Gravel
- ☐ Trees ☐ Lawn
- ☐ Pet Friendly
- ☐ Firewood
- ☐ Quiet ☐ Noisy

Cell Service / Carrier: _____
- ☐ Antenna Reception ☐ Satellite TV ☐ Cable TV
- ☐ Wifi Available ☐ Free ☐ Fee $_____

Memberships: _____

Ammenities: _____

Location	☺	😐	☹	Water Pressure	☺	😐	☹
Restrooms	☺	😐	☹	Laundry	☺	😐	☹
Pool	☺	😐	☹	Hot Tub	☺	😐	☹

PLACES VISITED / ACTIVITIES: _____
_____
_____
_____

PEOPLE MET / NEW FRIENDS: _____
_____
_____
_____

FOOD, DINING & RESTAURANTS: _____
_____
_____
_____

HIGHLIGHTS / MEMORABLE EVENTS: _____
_____
_____
_____

PLACES TO GO & THINGS TO DO FOR NEXT TIME: _____
_____
_____
_____

NOTES:

Date: _____

From: _____

To: _____

Route Taken: _____
_____

Weather:

Beginning Mileage: _____

Ending Mileage: _____

Total Miles Traveled: _____

Campground Information

Name: _____

Address: _____

Phone: _____

Site # _____ $ _____ ☐ Day ☐ Week ☐ Month

☐ First Visit ☐ Return Visit ☐ Easy Access
☐ Site Level ☐ Back-in ☐ Pull-through
☐ 15 amp ☐ 30 amp ☐ 50 amp
☐ Water ☐ Sewer ☐ Shade ☐ Sun
☐ Paved ☐ Sand / Grass ☐ Gravel
☐ Picnic Table ☐ Fire ring ☐ Trees ☐ Lawn
☐ Patio ☐ Kid Friendly ☐ Pet Friendly
☐ Store ☐ Cafe ☐ Firewood
☐ Ice ☐ Secuiryt ☐ Quiet ☐ Noisy

Our Rating: ☆ ☆ ☆ ☆ ☆

GPS: _____

Altitude: _____

Cell Service / Carrier: _____

☐ Antenna Reception ☐ Satellite TV ☐ Cable TV
☐ Wifi Available ☐ Free ☐ Fee $ _____

Memberships: _____

Ammenities: _____

Location   ☺ 😐 ☹   Water Pressure ☺ 😐 ☹
Restrooms   ☺ 😐 ☹   Laundry   ☺ 😐 ☹
Pool   ☺ 😐 ☹   Hot Tub   ☺ 😐 ☹

Places Visited / Activities: _____
_____
_____
_____

People Met / New Friends: _____
_____
_____
_____

Food, Dining & Restaurants: _____
_____
_____
_____

Highlights / Memorable Events: _____
_____
_____
_____

Places To Go & Things To Do for Next Time: _____
_____
_____
_____

NOTES:

Date: _____
Weather:
From: _____
To: _____
Route Taken: _____
_____

Beginning Mileage: _____
Ending Mileage: _____
Total Miles Traveled: _____

Campground Information

Name: _____
Address: _____
Phone: _____

Site # _____ $ _____ ☐ Day ☐ Week ☐ Month
- ☐ First Visit
- ☐ Site Level
- ☐ 15 amp
- ☐ Water
- ☐ Paved
- ☐ Picnic Table
- ☐ Patio
- ☐ Store
- ☐ Ice

- ☐ Return Visit
- ☐ Back-in
- ☐ 30 amp
- ☐ Sewer
- ☐ Sand / Grass
- ☐ Fire ring
- ☐ Kid Friendly
- ☐ Cafe
- ☐ Secuiryt

- ☐ Easy Access
- ☐ Pull-through
- ☐ 50 amp
- ☐ Shade ☐ Sun
- ☐ Gravel
- ☐ Trees ☐ Lawn
- ☐ Pet Friendly
- ☐ Firewood
- ☐ Quiet ☐ Noisy

Our Rating: ☆ ☆ ☆ ☆ ☆
GPS: _____
Altitude: _____
Cell Service / Carrier: _____
- ☐ Antenna Reception
- ☐ Wifi Available
- ☐ Satellite TV
- ☐ Cable TV
- ☐ Free ☐ Fee $ _____

Memberships: _____
Ammenities: _____

	☺ ☹ ☺		☺ ☹ ☺
Location	☺ ☹ ☺	Water Pressure	☺ ☹ ☺
Restrooms	☺ ☹ ☺	Laundry	☺ ☹ ☺
Pool	☺ ☹ ☺	Hot Tub	☺ ☹ ☺

Places Visited / Activities: _____
_____
_____
_____

People Met / New Friends: _____
_____
_____
_____

Food, Dining & Restaurants: _____
_____
_____
_____

Highlights / Memorable Events: _____
_____
_____
_____

Places To Go & Things To Do for Next Time: _____
_____
_____
_____

Notes:

Date: _____

Weather:

From: _____

To: _____

Route Taken: _____

_____

Beginning Mileage: _____

Ending Mileage: _____

Total Miles Traveled: _____

Campground Information

Name: _____

Address: _____

Phone: _____

Site # _____ $ _____ ☐ Day ☐ Week ☐ Month

☐ First Visit ☐ Return Visit ☐ Easy Access
☐ Site Level ☐ Back-in ☐ Pull-through
☐ 15 amp ☐ 30 amp ☐ 50 amp
☐ Water ☐ Sewer ☐ Shade ☐ Sun
☐ Paved ☐ Sand / Grass ☐ Gravel
☐ Picnic Table ☐ Fire ring ☐ Trees ☐ Lawn
☐ Patio ☐ Kid Friendly ☐ Pet Friendly
☐ Store ☐ Cafe ☐ Firewood
☐ Ice ☐ Secuiryt ☐ Quiet ☐ Noisy

Our Rating: ☆ ☆ ☆ ☆ ☆

GPS: _____

Altitude: _____

Cell Service / Carrier: _____

☐ Antenna Reception ☐ Satellite TV ☐ Cable TV
☐ Wifi Available ☐ Free ☐ Fee $_____

Memberships: _____

Ammenities: _____

Location	☺	😐	☹	Water Pressure	☺	😐	☹
Restrooms	☺	😐	☹	Laundry	☺	😐	☹
Pool	☺	😐	☹	Hot Tub	☺	😐	☹

Places Visited / Activities: _____

_____

_____

People Met / New Friends: _____

_____

_____

Food, Dining & Restaurants: _____

_____

_____

Highlights / Memorable Events: _____

_____

_____

Places To Go & Things To Do for Next Time: _____

_____

_____

NOTES:

Date: _____

Weather:

From: _____

To: _____

Route Taken: _____
_____

Beginning Mileage: _____

Ending Mileage: _____

Total Miles Traveled: _____

Campground Information

Name: _____
Address: _____
Phone: _____

Site # _____ $ _____ ☐ Day ☐ Week ☐ Month
- ☐ First Visit
- ☐ Site Level
- ☐ 15 amp
- ☐ Water
- ☐ Paved
- ☐ Picnic Table
- ☐ Patio
- ☐ Store
- ☐ Ice

- ☐ Return Visit
- ☐ Back-in
- ☐ 30 amp
- ☐ Sewer
- ☐ Sand / Grass
- ☐ Fire ring
- ☐ Kid Friendly
- ☐ Cafe
- ☐ Secuiryt

- ☐ Easy Access
- ☐ Pull-through
- ☐ 50 amp
- ☐ Shade ☐ Sun
- ☐ Gravel
- ☐ Trees ☐ Lawn
- ☐ Pet Friendly
- ☐ Firewood
- ☐ Quiet ☐ Noisy

Our Rating: ☆ ☆ ☆ ☆ ☆
GPS: _____
Altitude: _____
Cell Service / Carrier: _____
- ☐ Antenna Reception ☐ Satellite TV ☐ Cable TV
- ☐ Wifi Available ☐ Free ☐ Fee $_____

Memberships: _____
Ammenities: _____

Location	☺	😐	☹	Water Pressure	☺	😐	☹
Restrooms	☺	😐	☹	Laundry	☺	😐	☹
Pool	☺	😐	☹	Hot Tub	☺	😐	☹

Places Visited / Activities: _____
_____
_____
_____

People Met / New Friends: _____
_____
_____
_____

Food, Dining & Restaurants: _____
_____
_____
_____

Highlights / Memorable Events: _____
_____
_____
_____

Places To Go & Things To Do for Next Time: _____
_____
_____
_____

Notes:

Date: _____

Weather:

From: _____
To: _____
Route Taken: _____
_____

Beginning Mileage: _____
Ending Mileage: _____
Total Miles Traveled: _____

Campground Information

Name: _____
Address: _____
Phone: _____

Site # _____ $ _____ ☐ Day ☐ Week ☐ Month

☐ First Visit   ☐ Return Visit   ☐ Easy Access
☐ Site Level   ☐ Back-in   ☐ Pull-through
☐ 15 amp   ☐ 30 amp   ☐ 50 amp
☐ Water   ☐ Sewer   ☐ Shade   ☐ Sun
☐ Paved   ☐ Sand / Grass   ☐ Gravel
☐ Picnic Table   ☐ Fire ring   ☐ Trees   ☐ Lawn
☐ Patio   ☐ Kid Friendly   ☐ Pet Friendly
☐ Store   ☐ Cafe   ☐ Firewood
☐ Ice   ☐ Secuiryt   ☐ Quiet   ☐ Noisy

Our Rating: ☆ ☆ ☆ ☆ ☆
GPS: _____
Altitude: _____
Cell Service / Carrier: _____

☐ Antenna Reception   ☐ Satellite TV   ☐ Cable TV
☐ Wifi Available   ☐ Free ☐ Fee $_____

Memberships: _____
Ammenities: _____

Location	☺ ☹ ☹	Water Pressure	☺ ☹ ☹
Restrooms	☺ ☹ ☹	Laundry	☺ ☹ ☹
Pool	☺ ☹ ☹	Hot Tub	☺ ☹ ☹

Places Visited / Activities:
_____
_____
_____
_____

People Met / New Friends:
_____
_____
_____
_____

Food, Dining & Restaurants:
_____
_____
_____
_____

Highlights / Memorable Events:
_____
_____
_____

Places To Go & Things To Do for Next Time:
_____
_____
_____
_____

Notes:

Date: _____

Weather:

From: _____

To: _____

Route Taken: _____

_____

Beginning Mileage: _____

Ending Mileage: _____

Total Miles Traveled: _____

Campground Information

Name: _____

Address: _____

Phone: _____

Site # _____ $ _____ ☐ Day ☐ Week ☐ Month

- ☐ First Visit
- ☐ Site Level
- ☐ 15 amp
- ☐ Water
- ☐ Paved
- ☐ Picnic Table
- ☐ Patio
- ☐ Store
- ☐ Ice

- ☐ Return Visit
- ☐ Back-in
- ☐ 30 amp
- ☐ Sewer
- ☐ Sand / Grass
- ☐ Fire ring
- ☐ Kid Friendly
- ☐ Cafe
- ☐ Secuiryt

- ☐ Easy Access
- ☐ Pull-through
- ☐ 50 amp
- ☐ Shade ☐ Sun
- ☐ Gravel
- ☐ Trees ☐ Lawn
- ☐ Pet Friendly
- ☐ Firewood
- ☐ Quiet ☐ Noisy

Our Rating: ☆ ☆ ☆ ☆ ☆

GPS: _____

Altitude: _____

Cell Service / Carrier: _____

- ☐ Antenna Reception   ☐ Satellite TV   ☐ Cable TV
- ☐ Wifi Available   ☐ Free ☐ Fee $_____

Memberships: _____

Ammenities: _____

Location	☺	😐	☹	Water Pressure	☺	😐	☹
Restrooms	☺	😐	☹	Laundry	☺	😐	☹
Pool	☺	😐	☹	Hot Tub	☺	😐	☹

Places Visited / Activities:

_____
_____
_____
_____

People Met / New Friends:

_____
_____
_____
_____

Food, Dining & Restaurants:

_____
_____
_____
_____

Highlights / Memorable Events:

_____
_____
_____
_____

Places To Go & Things To Do for Next Time:

_____
_____
_____
_____

NOTES:

Date: _____
Weather:

From: _____
To: _____
Route Taken: _____
_____

Beginning Mileage: _____
Ending Mileage: _____
Total Miles Traveled: _____

Campground Information

Name: _____
Address: _____
Phone: _____

Site #_____ $_____ ☐ Day ☐ Week ☐ Month
- ☐ First Visit
- ☐ Site Level
- ☐ 15 amp
- ☐ Water
- ☐ Paved
- ☐ Picnic Table
- ☐ Patio
- ☐ Store
- ☐ Ice

- ☐ Return Visit
- ☐ Back-in
- ☐ 30 amp
- ☐ Sewer
- ☐ Sand / Grass
- ☐ Fire ring
- ☐ Kid Friendly
- ☐ Cafe
- ☐ Secuiryt

- ☐ Easy Access
- ☐ Pull-through
- ☐ 50 amp
- ☐ Shade ☐ Sun
- ☐ Gravel
- ☐ Trees ☐ Lawn
- ☐ Pet Friendly
- ☐ Firewood
- ☐ Quiet ☐ Noisy

Our Rating: ☆ ☆ ☆ ☆ ☆
GPS: _____
Altitude: _____
Cell Service / Carrier: _____
- ☐ Antenna Reception ☐ Satellite TV ☐ Cable TV
- ☐ Wifi Available ☐ Free ☐ Fee $_____
Memberships: _____
Ammenities: _____

Location	☺	😐	☹	Water Pressure	☺	😐	☹
Restrooms	☺	😐	☹	Laundry	☺	😐	☹
Pool	☺	😐	☹	Hot Tub	☺	😐	☹

Places Visited / Activities: _____
_____
_____
_____

People Met / New Friends: _____
_____
_____
_____

Food, Dining & Restaurants: _____
_____
_____
_____

Highlights / Memorable Events: _____
_____
_____
_____

Places To Go & Things To Do for Next Time: _____
_____
_____
_____

NOTES:

Date: _____ From: _____ Beginning Mileage: _____

Weather: To: _____ Ending Mileage: _____

Route Taken: _____

_____ Total Miles Traveled: _____

Campground Information

Name: _____

Address: _____

Phone: _____

Our Rating: ☆ ☆ ☆ ☆ ☆

GPS: _____

Altitude: _____

Site # _____ $ _____ ☐ Day ☐ Week ☐ Month

- ☐ First Visit ☐ Return Visit ☐ Easy Access
- ☐ Site Level ☐ Back-in ☐ Pull-through
- ☐ 15 amp ☐ 30 amp ☐ 50 amp
- ☐ Water ☐ Sewer ☐ Shade ☐ Sun
- ☐ Paved ☐ Sand / Grass ☐ Gravel
- ☐ Picnic Table ☐ Fire ring ☐ Trees ☐ Lawn
- ☐ Patio ☐ Kid Friendly ☐ Pet Friendly
- ☐ Store ☐ Cafe ☐ Firewood
- ☐ Ice ☐ Secuiryt ☐ Quiet ☐ Noisy

Cell Service / Carrier: _____

- ☐ Antenna Reception ☐ Satellite TV ☐ Cable TV
- ☐ Wifi Available ☐ Free ☐ Fee $_____

Memberships: _____

Ammenities: _____

Location	☺	😐	☹	Water Pressure	☺	😐	☹
Restrooms	☺	😐	☹	Laundry	☺	😐	☹
Pool	☺	😐	☹	Hot Tub	☺	😐	☹

Places Visited / Activities: _____

_____

_____

_____

People Met / New Friends: _____

_____

_____

_____

Food, Dining & Restaurants: _____

_____

_____

_____

Highlights / Memorable Events: _____

_____

_____

_____

Places To Go & Things To Do for Next Time: _____

_____

_____

_____

Notes:

Date: _____	From: _____
Weather:	To: _____
☀ ⛅ ☂ ❄ 🌡 🌡 📢 ☁	Route Taken: _____

Beginning Mileage: _____

Ending Mileage: _____

Total Miles Traveled: _____

Campground Information

Name: _____

Address: _____

Phone: _____

Site # _____ $ _____ ☐ Day ☐ Week ☐ Month

☐ First Visit ☐ Return Visit ☐ Easy Access
☐ Site Level ☐ Back-in ☐ Pull-through
☐ 15 amp ☐ 30 amp ☐ 50 amp
☐ Water ☐ Sewer ☐ Shade ☐ Sun
☐ Paved ☐ Sand / Grass ☐ Gravel
☐ Picnic Table ☐ Fire ring ☐ Trees ☐ Lawn
☐ Patio ☐ Kid Friendly ☐ Pet Friendly
☐ Store ☐ Cafe ☐ Firewood
☐ Ice ☐ Secuiryt ☐ Quiet ☐ Noisy

Our Rating: ☆ ☆ ☆ ☆ ☆

GPS: _____

Altitude: _____

Cell Service / Carrier: _____

☐ Antenna Reception ☐ Satellite TV ☐ Cable TV
☐ Wifi Available ☐ Free ☐ Fee $ _____

Memberships: _____

Ammenities: _____

Location	🙂	😐	☹	Water Pressure	🙂	😐	☹
Restrooms	🙂	😐	☹	Laundry	🙂	😐	☹
Pool	🙂	😐	☹	Hot Tub	🙂	😐	☹

Places Visited / Activities: _____

_____

_____

People Met / New Friends: _____

_____

_____

Food, Dining & Restaurants: _____

_____

_____

Highlights / Memorable Events: _____

_____

_____

Places To Go & Things To Do for Next Time: _____

_____

_____

NOTES:

Date: _____
Weather:

From: _____
To: _____
Route Taken: _____
_____

Beginning Mileage: _____
Ending Mileage: _____
Total Miles Traveled: _____

Campground Information

Name: _____
Address: _____
Phone: _____

Site # _____ $ _____ ☐ Day ☐ Week ☐ Month
☐ First Visit   ☐ Return Visit   ☐ Easy Access
☐ Site Level   ☐ Back-in   ☐ Pull-through
☐ 15 amp   ☐ 30 amp   ☐ 50 amp
☐ Water   ☐ Sewer   ☐ Shade   ☐ Sun
☐ Paved   ☐ Sand / Grass   ☐ Gravel
☐ Picnic Table ☐ Fire ring   ☐ Trees   ☐ Lawn
☐ Patio   ☐ Kid Friendly   ☐ Pet Friendly
☐ Store   ☐ Cafe   ☐ Firewood
☐ Ice   ☐ Secuiryt   ☐ Quiet   ☐ Noisy

Our Rating: ☆ ☆ ☆ ☆ ☆
GPS: _____
Altitude: _____
Cell Service / Carrier: _____
☐ Antenna Reception   ☐ Satellite TV   ☐ Cable TV
☐ Wifi Available   ☐ Free   ☐ Fee $_____
Memberships: _____
Ammenities: _____

Location	☺	😐	☹	Water Pressure	☺	😐	☹
Restrooms	☺	😐	☹	Laundry	☺	😐	☹
Pool	☺	😐	☹	Hot Tub	☺	😐	☹

Places Visited / Activities: _____
_____
_____
_____

People Met / New Friends: _____
_____
_____
_____

Food, Dining & Restaurants: _____
_____
_____
_____

Highlights / Memorable Events: _____
_____
_____
_____

Places To Go & Things To Do for Next Time: _____
_____
_____
_____

NOTES:

Date: _____

Weather:

From: _____

To: _____

Route Taken: _____
_____

Beginning Mileage: _____

Ending Mileage: _____

Total Miles Traveled: _____

Campground Information

Name: _____

Address: _____

Phone: _____

Our Rating: ☆ ☆ ☆ ☆ ☆

GPS: _____

Altitude: _____

Site # _____ $ _____ ☐ Day ☐ Week ☐ Month

- ☐ First Visit
- ☐ Site Level
- ☐ 15 amp
- ☐ Water
- ☐ Paved
- ☐ Picnic Table
- ☐ Patio
- ☐ Store
- ☐ Ice

- ☐ Return Visit
- ☐ Back-in
- ☐ 30 amp
- ☐ Sewer
- ☐ Sand / Grass
- ☐ Fire ring
- ☐ Kid Friendly
- ☐ Cafe
- ☐ Secuiryt

- ☐ Easy Access
- ☐ Pull-through
- ☐ 50 amp
- ☐ Shade ☐ Sun
- ☐ Gravel
- ☐ Trees ☐ Lawn
- ☐ Pet Friendly
- ☐ Firewood
- ☐ Quiet ☐ Noisy

Cell Service / Carrier: _____

- ☐ Antenna Reception
- ☐ Wifi Available
- ☐ Satellite TV
- ☐ Free ☐ Fee $_____
- ☐ Cable TV

Memberships: _____

Ammenities: _____

Location	☺	😐	☹	Water Pressure	☺	😐	☹
Restrooms	☺	😐	☹	Laundry	☺	😐	☹
Pool	☺	😐	☹	Hot Tub	☺	😐	☹

Places Visited / Activities:
_____
_____
_____
_____

People Met / New Friends:
_____
_____
_____
_____

Food, Dining & Restaurants:
_____
_____
_____
_____

Highlights / Memorable Events:
_____
_____
_____
_____

Places To Go & Things To Do for Next Time:
_____
_____
_____
_____

Notes:

Date: _____
Weather:

From: _____
To: _____
Route Taken: _____
_____

Beginning Mileage: _____
Ending Mileage: _____
Total Miles Traveled: _____

CAMPGROUND INFORMATION

Name: _____
Address: _____
Phone: _____

Our Rating: ☆ ☆ ☆ ☆ ☆
GPS: _____
Altitude: _____

Site # _____ $ _____ ☐ Day ☐ Week ☐ Month

Cell Service / Carrier: _____

☐ First Visit   ☐ Return Visit   ☐ Easy Access
☐ Site Level   ☐ Back-in   ☐ Pull-through
☐ 15 amp   ☐ 30 amp   ☐ 50 amp
☐ Water   ☐ Sewer   ☐ Shade   ☐ Sun
☐ Paved   ☐ Sand / Grass   ☐ Gravel
☐ Picnic Table   ☐ Fire ring   ☐ Trees   ☐ Lawn
☐ Patio   ☐ Kid Friendly   ☐ Pet Friendly
☐ Store   ☐ Cafe   ☐ Firewood
☐ Ice   ☐ Secuiryt   ☐ Quiet   ☐ Noisy

☐ Antenna Reception   ☐ Satellite TV   ☐ Cable TV
☐ Wifi Available   ☐ Free ☐ Fee $_____
Memberships: _____
Ammenities: _____

Location   ☺ ☹ ☹   Water Pressure   ☺ ☹ ☹
Restrooms ☺ ☹ ☹   Laundry   ☺ ☹ ☹
Pool   ☺ ☹ ☹   Hot Tub   ☺ ☹ ☹

PLACES VISITED / ACTIVITIES: _____
_____
_____
_____

PEOPLE MET / NEW FRIENDS: _____
_____
_____
_____

FOOD, DINING & RESTAURANTS: _____
_____
_____
_____

HIGHLIGHTS / MEMORABLE EVENTS: _____
_____
_____
_____

PLACES TO GO & THINGS TO DO FOR NEXT TIME: _____
_____
_____
_____

NOTES:

Date: _____	From: _____	Beginning Mileage: _____
Weather: ☀ ⛅ ☔ ❄ 🌡 🌡 📢 💨	To: _____ Route Taken: _____	Ending Mileage: _____ Total Miles Traveled: _____

CAMPGROUND INFORMATION

Name: _____

Address: _____

Phone: _____

Our Rating: ☆ ☆ ☆ ☆ ☆

GPS: _____

Altitude: _____

Site # _____ $ _____ ☐ Day ☐ Week ☐ Month

Cell Service / Carrier: _____

- ☐ First Visit
- ☐ Site Level
- ☐ 15 amp
- ☐ Water
- ☐ Paved
- ☐ Picnic Table
- ☐ Patio
- ☐ Store
- ☐ Ice

- ☐ Return Visit
- ☐ Back-in
- ☐ 30 amp
- ☐ Sewer
- ☐ Sand / Grass
- ☐ Fire ring
- ☐ Kid Friendly
- ☐ Cafe
- ☐ Secuiryt

- ☐ Easy Access
- ☐ Pull-through
- ☐ 50 amp
- ☐ Shade ☐ Sun
- ☐ Gravel
- ☐ Trees ☐ Lawn
- ☐ Pet Friendly
- ☐ Firewood
- ☐ Quiet ☐ Noisy

- ☐ Antenna Reception ☐ Satellite TV ☐ Cable TV
- ☐ Wifi Available ☐ Free ☐ Fee $ _____

Memberships: _____

Ammenities: _____

Location	🙂	😐	🙁	Water Pressure	🙂	😐	🙁
Restrooms	🙂	😐	🙁	Laundry	🙂	😐	🙁
Pool	🙂	😐	🙁	Hot Tub	🙂	😐	🙁

PLACES VISITED / ACTIVITIES: _____

PEOPLE MET / NEW FRIENDS: _____

FOOD, DINING & RESTAURANTS: _____

HIGHLIGHTS / MEMORABLE EVENTS: _____

PLACES TO GO & THINGS TO DO FOR NEXT TIME: _____

NOTES:

Date: _____ From: _____ Beginning Mileage: _____

Weather: To: _____ Ending Mileage: _____

Route Taken: _____

_____ Total Miles Traveled: _____

Campground Information

Name: _____

Address: _____

Phone: _____

Site # _____ $ _____ ☐ Day ☐ Week ☐ Month

☐ First Visit   ☐ Return Visit   ☐ Easy Access
☐ Site Level   ☐ Back-in   ☐ Pull-through
☐ 15 amp   ☐ 30 amp   ☐ 50 amp
☐ Water   ☐ Sewer   ☐ Shade   ☐ Sun
☐ Paved   ☐ Sand / Grass   ☐ Gravel
☐ Picnic Table   ☐ Fire ring   ☐ Trees   ☐ Lawn
☐ Patio   ☐ Kid Friendly   ☐ Pet Friendly
☐ Store   ☐ Cafe   ☐ Firewood
☐ Ice   ☐ Secuiryt   ☐ Quiet   ☐ Noisy

Our Rating: ☆ ☆ ☆ ☆ ☆

GPS: _____

Altitude: _____

Cell Service / Carrier: _____

☐ Antenna Reception   ☐ Satellite TV   ☐ Cable TV
☐ Wifi Available   ☐ Free ☐ Fee $_____

Memberships: _____

Ammenities: _____

Location   ☺ ☺ ☹   Water Pressure ☺ ☺ ☹
Restrooms ☺ ☺ ☹   Laundry   ☺ ☺ ☹
Pool   ☺ ☺ ☹   Hot Tub   ☺ ☺ ☹

Places Visited / Activities: _____

People Met / New Friends: _____

Food, Dining & Restaurants: _____

Highlights / Memorable Events: _____

Places To Go & Things To Do for Next Time: _____

NOTES:

Date: _____

Weather:

From: _____
To: _____
Route Taken: _____
_____

Beginning Mileage: _____

Ending Mileage: _____

Total Miles Traveled: _____

Campground Information

Name: _____
Address: _____
Phone: _____

Site # _____ $ _____ ☐ Day ☐ Week ☐ Month

☐ First Visit ☐ Return Visit ☐ Easy Access
☐ Site Level ☐ Back-in ☐ Pull-through
☐ 15 amp ☐ 30 amp ☐ 50 amp
☐ Water ☐ Sewer ☐ Shade ☐ Sun
☐ Paved ☐ Sand / Grass ☐ Gravel
☐ Picnic Table ☐ Fire ring ☐ Trees ☐ Lawn
☐ Patio ☐ Kid Friendly ☐ Pet Friendly
☐ Store ☐ Cafe ☐ Firewood
☐ Ice ☐ Secuiryt ☐ Quiet ☐ Noisy

Our Rating: ☆ ☆ ☆ ☆ ☆
GPS: _____
Altitude: _____
Cell Service / Carrier: _____
☐ Antenna Reception ☐ Satellite TV ☐ Cable TV
☐ Wifi Available ☐ Free ☐ Fee $ _____
Memberships: _____
Ammenities: _____

Location	☺	😐	☹	Water Pressure	☺	😐	☹
Restrooms	☺	😐	☹	Laundry	☺	😐	☹
Pool	☺	😐	☹	Hot Tub	☺	😐	☹

Places Visited / Activities: _____
_____
_____
_____

People Met / New Friends: _____
_____
_____
_____

Food, Dining & Restaurants: _____
_____
_____
_____

Highlights / Memorable Events: _____
_____
_____
_____

Places To Go & Things To Do for Next Time: _____
_____
_____
_____

NOTES:

Date: _____
From: _____
To: _____
Route Taken: _____
_____

Weather:

Beginning Mileage: _____
Ending Mileage: _____
Total Miles Traveled: _____

Campground Information

Name: _____
Address: _____
Phone: _____

Our Rating: ☆ ☆ ☆ ☆ ☆
GPS: _____
Altitude: _____

Site # _____ $ _____ ☐ Day ☐ Week ☐ Month
☐ First Visit ☐ Return Visit ☐ Easy Access
☐ Site Level ☐ Back-in ☐ Pull-through
☐ 15 amp ☐ 30 amp ☐ 50 amp
☐ Water ☐ Sewer ☐ Shade ☐ Sun
☐ Paved ☐ Sand / Grass ☐ Gravel
☐ Picnic Table ☐ Fire ring ☐ Trees ☐ Lawn
☐ Patio ☐ Kid Friendly ☐ Pet Friendly
☐ Store ☐ Cafe ☐ Firewood
☐ Ice ☐ Secuiryt ☐ Quiet ☐ Noisy

Cell Service / Carrier: _____
☐ Antenna Reception ☐ Satellite TV ☐ Cable TV
☐ Wifi Available ☐ Free ☐ Fee $ _____
Memberships: _____
Ammenities: _____

Location	☺	😐	☹	Water Pressure	☺	😐	☹
Restrooms	☺	😐	☹	Laundry	☺	😐	☹
Pool	☺	😐	☹	Hot Tub	☺	😐	☹

Places Visited / Activities:
_____
_____
_____

People Met / New Friends:
_____
_____
_____

Food, Dining & Restaurants:
_____
_____
_____

Highlights / Memorable Events:
_____
_____
_____

Places To Go & Things To Do for Next Time:
_____
_____
_____

NOTES:

Date: _____

Weather:

From: _____
To: _____
Route Taken: _____
_____

Beginning Mileage: _____
Ending Mileage: _____
Total Miles Traveled: _____

Campground Information

Name: _____
Address: _____
Phone: _____

Our Rating: ☆ ☆ ☆ ☆
GPS: _____
Altitude: _____

Site #_____ $_____ ☐ Day ☐ Week ☐ Month

- ☐ First Visit
- ☐ Site Level
- ☐ 15 amp
- ☐ Water
- ☐ Paved
- ☐ Picnic Table
- ☐ Patio
- ☐ Store
- ☐ Ice

- ☐ Return Visit
- ☐ Back-in
- ☐ 30 amp
- ☐ Sewer
- ☐ Sand / Grass
- ☐ Fire ring
- ☐ Kid Friendly
- ☐ Cafe
- ☐ Secuiryt

- ☐ Easy Access
- ☐ Pull-through
- ☐ 50 amp
- ☐ Shade ☐ Sun
- ☐ Gravel
- ☐ Trees ☐ Lawn
- ☐ Pet Friendly
- ☐ Firewood
- ☐ Quiet ☐ Noisy

Cell Service / Carrier: _____
☐ Antenna Reception ☐ Satellite TV ☐ Cable TV
☐ Wifi Available ☐ Free ☐ Fee $_____
Memberships: _____
Ammenities: _____

	☺ ☺ ☹		☺ ☺ ☹
Location	☺ ☺ ☹	Water Pressure	☺ ☺ ☹
Restrooms	☺ ☺ ☹	Laundry	☺ ☺ ☹
Pool	☺ ☺ ☹	Hot Tub	☺ ☺ ☹

Places Visited / Activities:
_____
_____
_____

People Met / New Friends:
_____
_____
_____

Food, Dining & Restaurants:
_____
_____
_____

Highlights / Memorable Events:
_____
_____
_____

Places To Go & Things To Do for Next Time:
_____
_____
_____

NOTES:

Date: _____

From: _____

To: _____

Route Taken: _____

_____

Weather:

Beginning Mileage: _____

Ending Mileage: _____

Total Miles Traveled: _____

Campground Information

Name: _____

Address: _____

Phone: _____

Site #_____ $_____

- [ ] Day [ ] Week [ ] Month
- [ ] First Visit
- [ ] Site Level
- [ ] 15 amp
- [ ] Water
- [ ] Paved
- [ ] Picnic Table
- [ ] Patio
- [ ] Store
- [ ] Ice
- [ ] Return Visit
- [ ] Back-in
- [ ] 30 amp
- [ ] Sewer
- [ ] Sand / Grass
- [ ] Fire ring
- [ ] Kid Friendly
- [ ] Cafe
- [ ] Secuiryt
- [ ] Easy Access
- [ ] Pull-through
- [ ] 50 amp
- [ ] Shade [ ] Sun
- [ ] Gravel
- [ ] Trees [ ] Lawn
- [ ] Pet Friendly
- [ ] Firewood
- [ ] Quiet [ ] Noisy

Our Rating: ☆ ☆ ☆ ☆ ☆

GPS: _____

Altitude: _____

Cell Service / Carrier: _____

- [ ] Antenna Reception
- [ ] Satellite TV
- [ ] Cable TV
- [ ] Wifi Available [ ] Free [ ] Fee $_____

Memberships: _____

Ammenities: _____

Location	☺	😐	☹	Water Pressure	☺	😐	☹
Restrooms	☺	😐	☹	Laundry	☺	😐	☹
Pool	☺	😐	☹	Hot Tub	☺	😐	☹

Places Visited / Activities: _____

_____

_____

_____

People Met / New Friends: _____

_____

_____

_____

Food, Dining & Restaurants: _____

_____

_____

_____

Highlights / Memorable Events: _____

_____

_____

_____

Places To Go & Things To Do for Next Time: _____

_____

_____

_____

Notes:

Date: _____
From: _____
Beginning Mileage: _____

Weather:
To: _____
Ending Mileage: _____

Route Taken: _____
_____
Total Miles Traveled: _____

Campground Information

Name: _____
Address: _____
Phone: _____

Our Rating: ☆ ☆ ☆ ☆ ☆
GPS: _____
Altitude: _____

Site # _____ $ _____ ☐ Day ☐ Week ☐ Month
Cell Service / Carrier: _____

- ☐ First Visit
- ☐ Site Level
- ☐ 15 amp
- ☐ Water
- ☐ Paved
- ☐ Picnic Table
- ☐ Patio
- ☐ Store
- ☐ Ice

- ☐ Return Visit
- ☐ Back-in
- ☐ 30 amp
- ☐ Sewer
- ☐ Sand / Grass
- ☐ Fire ring
- ☐ Kid Friendly
- ☐ Cafe
- ☐ Secuiryt

- ☐ Easy Access
- ☐ Pull-through
- ☐ 50 amp
- ☐ Shade ☐ Sun
- ☐ Gravel
- ☐ Trees ☐ Lawn
- ☐ Pet Friendly
- ☐ Firewood
- ☐ Quiet ☐ Noisy

- ☐ Antenna Reception ☐ Satellite TV ☐ Cable TV
- ☐ Wifi Available ☐ Free ☐ Fee $_____

Memberships: _____
Ammenities: _____

Location	☺	😐	☹	Water Pressure	☺	😐	☹
Restrooms	☺	😐	☹	Laundry	☺	😐	☹
Pool	☺	😐	☹	Hot Tub	☺	😐	☹

Places Visited / Activities: _____
_____
_____
_____

People Met / New Friends: _____
_____
_____
_____

Food, Dining & Restaurants: _____
_____
_____
_____

Highlights / Memorable Events: _____
_____
_____
_____

Places To Go & Things To Do for Next Time: _____
_____
_____
_____

NOTES:

Date: _____

Weather:

From: _____
To: _____
Route Taken: _____
_____

Beginning Mileage: _____

Ending Mileage: _____

Total Miles Traveled: _____

CAMPGROUND INFORMATION

Name: _____
Address: _____
Phone: _____

Site # _____ $ _____ ☐ Day ☐ Week ☐ Month

☐ First Visit   ☐ Return Visit   ☐ Easy Access
☐ Site Level   ☐ Back-in   ☐ Pull-through
☐ 15 amp   ☐ 30 amp   ☐ 50 amp
☐ Water   ☐ Sewer   ☐ Shade   ☐ Sun
☐ Paved   ☐ Sand / Grass   ☐ Gravel
☐ Picnic Table   ☐ Fire ring   ☐ Trees   ☐ Lawn
☐ Patio   ☐ Kid Friendly   ☐ Pet Friendly
☐ Store   ☐ Cafe   ☐ Firewood
☐ Ice   ☐ Secuiryt   ☐ Quiet   ☐ Noisy

Our Rating: ☆ ☆ ☆ ☆ ☆
GPS: _____
Altitude: _____
Cell Service / Carrier: _____
☐ Antenna Reception   ☐ Satellite TV   ☐ Cable TV
☐ Wifi Available   ☐ Free ☐ Fee $_____
Memberships: _____
Ammenities: _____

Location	☺	😐	☹	Water Pressure	☺	😐	☹
Restrooms	☺	😐	☹	Laundry	☺	😐	☹
Pool	☺	😐	☹	Hot Tub	☺	😐	☹

PLACES VISITED / ACTIVITIES: _____
_____
_____
_____

PEOPLE MET / NEW FRIENDS: _____
_____
_____
_____

FOOD, DINING & RESTAURANTS: _____
_____
_____
_____

HIGHLIGHTS / MEMORABLE EVENTS: _____
_____
_____
_____

PLACES TO GO & THINGS TO DO FOR NEXT TIME: _____
_____
_____
_____

Notes:

Date: _____

Weather:

From: _____

To: _____

Route Taken: _____

_____

Beginning Mileage: _____

Ending Mileage: _____

Total Miles Traveled: _____

Campground Information

Name: _____

Address: _____

Phone: _____

Our Rating: ☆ ☆ ☆ ☆ ☆

GPS: _____

Altitude: _____

Site # _____ $ _____
- [ ] Day [ ] Week [ ] Month
- [ ] First Visit
- [ ] Site Level
- [ ] 15 amp
- [ ] Water
- [ ] Paved
- [ ] Picnic Table
- [ ] Patio
- [ ] Store
- [ ] Ice
- [ ] Return Visit
- [ ] Back-in
- [ ] 30 amp
- [ ] Sewer
- [ ] Sand / Grass
- [ ] Fire ring
- [ ] Kid Friendly
- [ ] Cafe
- [ ] Secuiryt
- [ ] Easy Access
- [ ] Pull-through
- [ ] 50 amp
- [ ] Shade [ ] Sun
- [ ] Gravel
- [ ] Trees [ ] Lawn
- [ ] Pet Friendly
- [ ] Firewood
- [ ] Quiet [ ] Noisy

Cell Service / Carrier: _____

- [ ] Antenna Reception   [ ] Satellite TV   [ ] Cable TV
- [ ] Wifi Available   [ ] Free [ ] Fee $ _____

Memberships: _____

Ammenities: _____

	☺ 😐 ☹		☺ 😐 ☹
Location	☺ 😐 ☹	Water Pressure	☺ 😐 ☹
Restrooms	☺ 😐 ☹	Laundry	☺ 😐 ☹
Pool	☺ 😐 ☹	Hot Tub	☺ 😐 ☹

Places Visited / Activities: _____

_____

_____

_____

People Met / New Friends: _____

_____

_____

_____

Food, Dining & Restaurants: _____

_____

_____

_____

Highlights / Memorable Events: _____

_____

_____

_____

Places To Go & Things To Do for Next Time: _____

_____

_____

_____

Notes:

Date: _____

Weather:

From: _____
To: _____
Route Taken: _____
_____

Beginning Mileage: _____

Ending Mileage: _____

Total Miles Traveled: _____

Campground Information

Name: _____
Address: _____
Phone: _____

Site # _____ $ _____ ☐ Day ☐ Week ☐ Month

☐ First Visit   ☐ Return Visit   ☐ Easy Access
☐ Site Level   ☐ Back-in   ☐ Pull-through
☐ 15 amp   ☐ 30 amp   ☐ 50 amp
☐ Water   ☐ Sewer   ☐ Shade   ☐ Sun
☐ Paved   ☐ Sand / Grass   ☐ Gravel
☐ Picnic Table   ☐ Fire ring   ☐ Trees   ☐ Lawn
☐ Patio   ☐ Kid Friendly   ☐ Pet Friendly
☐ Store   ☐ Cafe   ☐ Firewood
☐ Ice   ☐ Secuiryt   ☐ Quiet   ☐ Noisy

Our Rating: ☆ ☆ ☆ ☆ ☆

GPS: _____
Altitude: _____
Cell Service / Carrier: _____
☐ Antenna Reception   ☐ Satellite TV   ☐ Cable TV
☐ Wifi Available   ☐ Free ☐ Fee $_____
Memberships: _____
Ammenities: _____

Location	☺	😐	☹	Water Pressure	☺	😐	☹
Restrooms	☺	😐	☹	Laundry	☺	😐	☹
Pool	☺	😐	☹	Hot Tub	☺	😐	☹

Places Visited / Activities: _____
_____
_____
_____

People Met / New Friends: _____
_____
_____
_____

Food, Dining & Restaurants: _____
_____
_____
_____

Highlights / Memorable Events: _____
_____
_____
_____

Places To Go & Things To Do for Next Time: _____
_____
_____
_____

Notes:

Date: _____
Weather:

From: _____
To: _____
Route Taken: _____
_____

Beginning Mileage: _____
Ending Mileage: _____
Total Miles Traveled: _____

Campground Information

Name: _____
Address: _____
Phone: _____

Our Rating: ☆ ☆ ☆ ☆ ☆
GPS: _____
Altitude: _____

Site # _____ $ _____ ☐ Day ☐ Week ☐ Month
- ☐ First Visit   ☐ Return Visit   ☐ Easy Access
- ☐ Site Level   ☐ Back-in   ☐ Pull-through
- ☐ 15 amp   ☐ 30 amp   ☐ 50 amp
- ☐ Water   ☐ Sewer   ☐ Shade   ☐ Sun
- ☐ Paved   ☐ Sand / Grass   ☐ Gravel
- ☐ Picnic Table   ☐ Fire ring   ☐ Trees   ☐ Lawn
- ☐ Patio   ☐ Kid Friendly   ☐ Pet Friendly
- ☐ Store   ☐ Cafe   ☐ Firewood
- ☐ Ice   ☐ Secuiryt   ☐ Quiet   ☐ Noisy

Cell Service / Carrier: _____
- ☐ Antenna Reception   ☐ Satellite TV   ☐ Cable TV
- ☐ Wifi Available   ☐ Free ☐ Fee $_____

Memberships: _____
Ammenities: _____

Location	☺	😐	☹	Water Pressure	☺	😐	☹
Restrooms	☺	😐	☹	Laundry	☺	😐	☹
Pool	☺	😐	☹	Hot Tub	☺	😐	☹

Places Visited / Activities: _____
_____
_____
_____

People Met / New Friends: _____
_____
_____
_____

Food, Dining & Restaurants: _____
_____
_____
_____

Highlights / Memorable Events: _____
_____
_____
_____

Places To Go & Things To Do for Next Time: _____
_____
_____
_____

Notes:

Date: _____ From: _____ Beginning Mileage: _____

Weather: ☀ ⛅ ☔ ❄ 🌡 🌡 📯 🌫 To: _____ Ending Mileage: _____

Route Taken: _____ Total Miles Traveled: _____
_____

Campground Information

Name: _____ Our Rating: ☆ ☆ ☆ ☆ ☆

Address: _____ GPS: _____

Phone: _____ Altitude: _____

Site # _____ $ _____ ☐ Day ☐ Week ☐ Month Cell Service / Carrier: _____

☐ First Visit   ☐ Return Visit   ☐ Easy Access   ☐ Antenna Reception   ☐ Satellite TV   ☐ Cable TV
☐ Site Level   ☐ Back-in   ☐ Pull-through   ☐ Wifi Available   ☐ Free ☐ Fee $_____
☐ 15 amp   ☐ 30 amp   ☐ 50 amp
☐ Water   ☐ Sewer   ☐ Shade ☐ Sun   Memberships: _____
☐ Paved   ☐ Sand / Grass   ☐ Gravel   Ammenities: _____
☐ Picnic Table   ☐ Fire ring   ☐ Trees ☐ Lawn   Location   ☺ 😐 ☹   Water Pressure ☺ 😐 ☹
☐ Patio   ☐ Kid Friendly   ☐ Pet Friendly   Restrooms ☺ 😐 ☹   Laundry   ☺ 😐 ☹
☐ Store   ☐ Cafe   ☐ Firewood   Pool   ☺ 😐 ☹   Hot Tub   ☺ 😐 ☹
☐ Ice   ☐ Secuiryt   ☐ Quiet ☐ Noisy

Places Visited / Activities: _____
_____
_____
_____

People Met / New Friends: _____
_____
_____
_____

Food, Dining & Restaurants: _____
_____
_____
_____

Highlights / Memorable Events: _____
_____
_____
_____

Places To Go & Things To Do for Next Time: _____
_____
_____
_____

Notes:

Date: _____

Weather:

From: _____
To: _____
Route Taken: _____
_____

Beginning Mileage: _____

Ending Mileage: _____

Total Miles Traveled: _____

Campground Information

Name: _____
Address: _____
Phone: _____

Site # _____ $ _____ ☐ Day ☐ Week ☐ Month

☐ First Visit	☐ Return Visit	☐ Easy Access
☐ Site Level	☐ Back-in	☐ Pull-through
☐ 15 amp	☐ 30 amp	☐ 50 amp
☐ Water	☐ Sewer	☐ Shade ☐ Sun
☐ Paved	☐ Sand / Grass	☐ Gravel
☐ Picnic Table	☐ Fire ring	☐ Trees ☐ Lawn
☐ Patio	☐ Kid Friendly	☐ Pet Friendly
☐ Store	☐ Cafe	☐ Firewood
☐ Ice	☐ Secuiryt	☐ Quiet ☐ Noisy

Our Rating: ☆ ☆ ☆ ☆ ☆

GPS: _____
Altitude: _____
Cell Service / Carrier: _____

☐ Antenna Reception   ☐ Satellite TV   ☐ Cable TV
☐ Wifi Available   ☐ Free ☐ Fee $_____

Memberships: _____
Ammenities: _____

Location	☺	😐	☹	Water Pressure	☺	😐	☹
Restrooms	☺	😐	☹	Laundry	☺	😐	☹
Pool	☺	😐	☹	Hot Tub	☺	😐	☹

Places Visited / Activities: _____
_____
_____
_____

People Met / New Friends: _____
_____
_____
_____

Food, Dining & Restaurants: _____
_____
_____
_____

Highlights / Memorable Events: _____
_____
_____
_____

Places To Go & Things To Do for Next Time: _____
_____
_____
_____

Notes:

Date: _____ From: _____ Beginning Mileage: _____

Weather: To: _____ Ending Mileage: _____

Route Taken: _____

_____ Total Miles Traveled: _____

Campground Information

Name: _____

Address: _____

Phone: _____

Site # _____ $ _____ ☐ Day ☐ Week ☐ Month

☐ First Visit   ☐ Return Visit   ☐ Easy Access
☐ Site Level   ☐ Back-in   ☐ Pull-through
☐ 15 amp   ☐ 30 amp   ☐ 50 amp
☐ Water   ☐ Sewer   ☐ Shade   ☐ Sun
☐ Paved   ☐ Sand / Grass   ☐ Gravel
☐ Picnic Table   ☐ Fire ring   ☐ Trees   ☐ Lawn
☐ Patio   ☐ Kid Friendly   ☐ Pet Friendly
☐ Store   ☐ Cafe   ☐ Firewood
☐ Ice   ☐ Secuiryt   ☐ Quiet   ☐ Noisy

Our Rating: ☆ ☆ ☆ ☆ ☆

GPS: _____

Altitude: _____

Cell Service / Carrier: _____

☐ Antenna Reception   ☐ Satellite TV   ☐ Cable TV
☐ Wifi Available   ☐ Free ☐ Fee $_____

Memberships: _____

Ammenities: _____

Location   ☺ 😐 ☹   Water Pressure ☺ 😐 ☹
Restrooms   ☺ 😐 ☹   Laundry   ☺ 😐 ☹
Pool   ☺ 😐 ☹   Hot Tub   ☺ 😐 ☹

Places Visited / Activities: _____

_____

_____

People Met / New Friends: _____

_____

_____

Food, Dining & Restaurants: _____

_____

_____

Highlights / Memorable Events: _____

_____

_____

Places To Go & Things To Do for Next Time: _____

_____

_____

Notes:

Date: _____

Weather:

From: _____

To: _____

Route Taken: _____

_____

Beginning Mileage: _____

Ending Mileage: _____

Total Miles Traveled: _____

CAMPGROUND INFORMATION

Name: _____

Address: _____

Phone: _____

Site #_____ $_____ ☐ Day ☐ Week ☐ Month

- ☐ First Visit
- ☐ Site Level
- ☐ 15 amp
- ☐ Water
- ☐ Paved
- ☐ Picnic Table
- ☐ Patio
- ☐ Store
- ☐ Ice

- ☐ Return Visit
- ☐ Back-in
- ☐ 30 amp
- ☐ Sewer
- ☐ Sand / Grass
- ☐ Fire ring
- ☐ Kid Friendly
- ☐ Cafe
- ☐ Secuiryt

- ☐ Easy Access
- ☐ Pull-through
- ☐ 50 amp
- ☐ Shade ☐ Sun
- ☐ Gravel
- ☐ Trees ☐ Lawn
- ☐ Pet Friendly
- ☐ Firewood
- ☐ Quiet ☐ Noisy

Our Rating: ☆ ☆ ☆ ☆ ☆

GPS: _____

Altitude: _____

Cell Service / Carrier: _____

- ☐ Antenna Reception
- ☐ Wifi Available

☐ Satellite TV   ☐ Cable TV
☐ Free ☐ Fee $_____

Memberships: _____

Ammenities: _____

	☺	😐	☹		☺	😐	☹
Location				Water Pressure			
Restrooms				Laundry			
Pool				Hot Tub			

PLACES VISITED / ACTIVITIES: _____

_____

_____

_____

PEOPLE MET / NEW FRIENDS: _____

_____

_____

_____

FOOD, DINING & RESTAURANTS: _____

_____

_____

_____

HIGHLIGHTS / MEMORABLE EVENTS: _____

_____

_____

_____

PLACES TO GO & THINGS TO DO FOR NEXT TIME: _____

_____

_____

_____

NOTES:

Date: _____

Weather:

From: _____
To: _____
Route Taken: _____
_____

Beginning Mileage: _____

Ending Mileage: _____

Total Miles Traveled: _____

Campground Information

Name: _____
Address: _____
Phone: _____

Our Rating: ☆ ☆ ☆ ☆ ☆
GPS: _____
Altitude: _____

Site # _____ $ _____ ☐ Day ☐ Week ☐ Month

☐ First Visit
☐ Site Level
☐ 15 amp
☐ Water
☐ Paved
☐ Picnic Table
☐ Patio
☐ Store
☐ Ice

☐ Return Visit
☐ Back-in
☐ 30 amp
☐ Sewer
☐ Sand / Grass
☐ Fire ring
☐ Kid Friendly
☐ Cafe
☐ Secuiryt

☐ Easy Access
☐ Pull-through
☐ 50 amp
☐ Shade ☐ Sun
☐ Gravel
☐ Trees ☐ Lawn
☐ Pet Friendly
☐ Firewood
☐ Quiet ☐ Noisy

Cell Service / Carrier: _____
☐ Antenna Reception   ☐ Satellite TV   ☐ Cable TV
☐ Wifi Available   ☐ Free ☐ Fee $ _____
Memberships: _____
Ammenities: _____

	☺ ☹ ☹		☺ ☹ ☹
Location	☺ ☹ ☹	Water Pressure	☺ ☹ ☹
Restrooms	☺ ☹ ☹	Laundry	☺ ☹ ☹
Pool	☺ ☹ ☹	Hot Tub	☺ ☹ ☹

Places Visited / Activities: _____
_____
_____
_____

People Met / New Friends: _____
_____
_____
_____

Food, Dining & Restaurants: _____
_____
_____
_____

Highlights / Memorable Events: _____
_____
_____
_____

Places To Go & Things To Do for Next Time: _____
_____
_____
_____

Notes:

Date: _____

Weather:

From: _____
To: _____
Route Taken: _____
_____

Beginning Mileage: _____
Ending Mileage: _____
Total Miles Traveled: _____

Campground Information

Name: _____
Address: _____
Phone: _____

Site # _____ $ _____ ☐ Day ☐ Week ☐ Month

☐ First Visit   ☐ Return Visit   ☐ Easy Access
☐ Site Level   ☐ Back-in   ☐ Pull-through
☐ 15 amp   ☐ 30 amp   ☐ 50 amp
☐ Water   ☐ Sewer   ☐ Shade   ☐ Sun
☐ Paved   ☐ Sand / Grass   ☐ Gravel
☐ Picnic Table   ☐ Fire ring   ☐ Trees   ☐ Lawn
☐ Patio   ☐ Kid Friendly   ☐ Pet Friendly
☐ Store   ☐ Cafe   ☐ Firewood
☐ Ice   ☐ Secuiryt   ☐ Quiet   ☐ Noisy

Our Rating: ☆ ☆ ☆ ☆ ☆
GPS: _____
Altitude: _____
Cell Service / Carrier: _____
☐ Antenna Reception ☐ Satellite TV ☐ Cable TV
☐ Wifi Available   ☐ Free ☐ Fee $_____
Memberships: _____
Ammenities: _____

Location	☺	😐	☹	Water Pressure	☺	😐	☹
Restrooms	☺	😐	☹	Laundry	☺	😐	☹
Pool	☺	😐	☹	Hot Tub	☺	😐	☹

Places Visited / Activities: _____
_____
_____
_____

People Met / New Friends: _____
_____
_____
_____

Food, Dining & Restaurants: _____
_____
_____
_____

Highlights / Memorable Events: _____
_____
_____
_____

Places To Go & Things To Do for Next Time: _____
_____
_____
_____

NOTES:

Date: _____ From: _____ Beginning Mileage: _____

Weather: ☀ ⛅ ☂ ❄ To: _____ Ending Mileage: _____
🌡 🧊 📣 💨 Route Taken: _____
_____ Total Miles Traveled: _____

Campground Information

Name: _____ Our Rating: ☆ ☆ ☆ ☆ ☆

Address: _____ GPS: _____

Phone: _____ Altitude: _____

Site # _____ $ _____ ☐ Day ☐ Week ☐ Month Cell Service / Carrier: _____

☐ First Visit   ☐ Return Visit   ☐ Easy Access   ☐ Antenna Reception   ☐ Satellite TV   ☐ Cable TV
☐ Site Level   ☐ Back-in   ☐ Pull-through   ☐ Wifi Available   ☐ Free ☐ Fee $_____
☐ 15 amp   ☐ 30 amp   ☐ 50 amp
☐ Water   ☐ Sewer   ☐ Shade ☐ Sun   Memberships: _____
☐ Paved   ☐ Sand / Grass   ☐ Gravel   Ammenities: _____
☐ Picnic Table   ☐ Fire ring   ☐ Trees ☐ Lawn   Location   ☺ 😐 ☹   Water Pressure ☺ 😐 ☹
☐ Patio   ☐ Kid Friendly   ☐ Pet Friendly   Restrooms   ☺ 😐 ☹   Laundry   ☺ 😐 ☹
☐ Store   ☐ Cafe   ☐ Firewood
☐ Ice   ☐ Secuiryt   ☐ Quiet ☐ Noisy   Pool   ☺ 😐 ☹   Hot Tub   ☺ 😐 ☹

Places Visited / Activities: _____
_____
_____
_____

People Met / New Friends: _____
_____
_____
_____

Food, Dining & Restaurants: _____
_____
_____
_____

Highlights / Memorable Events: _____
_____
_____
_____

Places To Go & Things To Do for Next Time: _____
_____
_____
_____

NOTES:

Date: _____
Weather:
From: _____
To: _____
Route Taken: _____
_____

Beginning Mileage: _____
Ending Mileage: _____
Total Miles Traveled: _____

Campground Information

Name: _____
Address: _____
Phone: _____

Site # _____ $ _____ ☐ Day ☐ Week ☐ Month
☐ First Visit   ☐ Return Visit   ☐ Easy Access
☐ Site Level   ☐ Back-in   ☐ Pull-through
☐ 15 amp   ☐ 30 amp   ☐ 50 amp
☐ Water   ☐ Sewer   ☐ Shade   ☐ Sun
☐ Paved   ☐ Sand / Grass   ☐ Gravel
☐ Picnic Table   ☐ Fire ring   ☐ Trees   ☐ Lawn
☐ Patio   ☐ Kid Friendly   ☐ Pet Friendly
☐ Store   ☐ Cafe   ☐ Firewood
☐ Ice   ☐ Secuiryt   ☐ Quiet   ☐ Noisy

Our Rating: ☆ ☆ ☆ ☆ ☆
GPS: _____
Altitude: _____
Cell Service / Carrier: _____
☐ Antenna Reception   ☐ Satellite TV   ☐ Cable TV
☐ Wifi Available   ☐ Free ☐ Fee $_____
Memberships: _____
Ammenities: _____

Location   ☺ ☻ ☹   Water Pressure   ☺ ☻ ☹
Restrooms   ☺ ☻ ☹   Laundry   ☺ ☻ ☹
Pool   ☺ ☻ ☹   Hot Tub   ☺ ☻ ☹

Places Visited / Activities: _____

_____
_____
_____

People Met / New Friends: _____

_____
_____
_____

Food, Dining & Restaurants: _____

_____
_____
_____

Highlights / Memorable Events: _____

_____
_____
_____

Places To Go & Things To Do for Next Time: ____

_____
_____
_____

NOTES:

Date: _____

Weather:

From: _____

To: _____

Route Taken: _____
_____

Beginning Mileage: _____

Ending Mileage: _____

Total Miles Traveled: _____

Campground Information

Name: _____

Address: _____

Phone: _____

Our Rating: ☆ ☆ ☆ ☆ ☆

GPS: _____

Altitude: _____

Site # _____ $ _____ ☐ Day ☐ Week ☐ Month

- ☐ First Visit
- ☐ Site Level
- ☐ 15 amp
- ☐ Water
- ☐ Paved
- ☐ Picnic Table
- ☐ Patio
- ☐ Store
- ☐ Ice

- ☐ Return Visit
- ☐ Back-in
- ☐ 30 amp
- ☐ Sewer
- ☐ Sand / Grass
- ☐ Fire ring
- ☐ Kid Friendly
- ☐ Cafe
- ☐ Secuiryt

- ☐ Easy Access
- ☐ Pull-through
- ☐ 50 amp
- ☐ Shade ☐ Sun
- ☐ Gravel
- ☐ Trees ☐ Lawn
- ☐ Pet Friendly
- ☐ Firewood
- ☐ Quiet ☐ Noisy

Cell Service / Carrier: _____

- ☐ Antenna Reception ☐ Satellite TV ☐ Cable TV
- ☐ Wifi Available ☐ Free ☐ Fee $ _____

Memberships: _____

Ammenities: _____

	☺	😐	☹		☺	😐	☹
Location				Water Pressure			
Restrooms				Laundry			
Pool				Hot Tub			

Places Visited / Activities:
_____
_____
_____
_____

People Met / New Friends:
_____
_____
_____
_____

Food, Dining & Restaurants:
_____
_____
_____
_____

Highlights / Memorable Events:
_____
_____
_____
_____

Places To Go & Things To Do for Next Time:
_____
_____
_____
_____

NOTES:

Date: _____

Weather:

From: _____
To: _____
Route Taken: _____
_____

Beginning Mileage: _____

Ending Mileage: _____

Total Miles Traveled: _____

CAMPGROUND INFORMATION

Name: _____
Address: _____
Phone: _____

Site # _____ $ _____ ☐ Day ☐ Week ☐ Month

☐ First Visit   ☐ Return Visit   ☐ Easy Access
☐ Site Level   ☐ Back-in   ☐ Pull-through
☐ 15 amp   ☐ 30 amp   ☐ 50 amp
☐ Water   ☐ Sewer   ☐ Shade   ☐ Sun
☐ Paved   ☐ Sand / Grass   ☐ Gravel
☐ Picnic Table   ☐ Fire ring   ☐ Trees   ☐ Lawn
☐ Patio   ☐ Kid Friendly   ☐ Pet Friendly
☐ Store   ☐ Cafe   ☐ Firewood
☐ Ice   ☐ Secuiryt   ☐ Quiet   ☐ Noisy

Our Rating: ☆ ☆ ☆ ☆ ☆

GPS: _____
Altitude: _____
Cell Service / Carrier: _____

☐ Antenna Reception   ☐ Satellite TV   ☐ Cable TV
☐ Wifi Available   ☐ Free ☐ Fee $_____

Memberships: _____
Ammenities: _____

Location	☺	😐	☹	Water Pressure	☺	😐	☹
Restrooms	☺	😐	☹	Laundry	☺	😐	☹
Pool	☺	😐	☹	Hot Tub	☺	😐	☹

PLACES VISITED / ACTIVITIES: _____

_____
_____
_____

PEOPLE MET / NEW FRIENDS: _____

_____
_____
_____

FOOD, DINING & RESTAURANTS: _____

_____
_____
_____

HIGHLIGHTS / MEMORABLE EVENTS: _____

_____
_____
_____

PLACES TO GO & THINGS TO DO FOR NEXT TIME: _____

_____
_____
_____

Notes:

Date: _____

Weather:

From: _____

To: _____

Route Taken: _____

_____

Beginning Mileage: _____

Ending Mileage: _____

Total Miles Traveled: _____

Campground Information

Name: _____

Address: _____

Phone: _____

Site # _____ $ _____ ☐ Day ☐ Week ☐ Month

☐ First Visit   ☐ Return Visit   ☐ Easy Access
☐ Site Level   ☐ Back-in   ☐ Pull-through
☐ 15 amp   ☐ 30 amp   ☐ 50 amp
☐ Water   ☐ Sewer   ☐ Shade   ☐ Sun
☐ Paved   ☐ Sand / Grass   ☐ Gravel
☐ Picnic Table   ☐ Fire ring   ☐ Trees   ☐ Lawn
☐ Patio   ☐ Kid Friendly   ☐ Pet Friendly
☐ Store   ☐ Cafe   ☐ Firewood
☐ Ice   ☐ Secuiryt   ☐ Quiet   ☐ Noisy

Our Rating: ☆ ☆ ☆ ☆ ☆

GPS: _____

Altitude: _____

Cell Service / Carrier: _____

☐ Antenna Reception   ☐ Satellite TV   ☐ Cable TV
☐ Wifi Available   ☐ Free ☐ Fee $ _____

Memberships: _____

Ammenities: _____

Location   ☺ 😐 ☹   Water Pressure   ☺ 😐 ☹
Restrooms   ☺ 😐 ☹   Laundry   ☺ 😐 ☹
Pool   ☺ 😐 ☹   Hot Tub   ☺ 😐 ☹

Places Visited / Activities:

_____
_____
_____

People Met / New Friends:

_____
_____
_____

Food, Dining & Restaurants:

_____
_____
_____

Highlights / Memorable Events:

_____
_____
_____

Places To Go & Things To Do for Next Time:

_____
_____
_____

NOTES:

Date: _____

Weather:

From: _____
To: _____
Route Taken: _____
_____

Beginning Mileage: _____
Ending Mileage: _____
Total Miles Traveled: _____

Campground Information

Name: _____
Address: _____
Phone: _____

Site # _____ $ _____ ☐ Day ☐ Week ☐ Month
☐ First Visit   ☐ Return Visit   ☐ Easy Access
☐ Site Level   ☐ Back-in   ☐ Pull-through
☐ 15 amp   ☐ 30 amp   ☐ 50 amp
☐ Water   ☐ Sewer   ☐ Shade   ☐ Sun
☐ Paved   ☐ Sand / Grass   ☐ Gravel
☐ Picnic Table   ☐ Fire ring   ☐ Trees   ☐ Lawn
☐ Patio   ☐ Kid Friendly   ☐ Pet Friendly
☐ Store   ☐ Cafe   ☐ Firewood
☐ Ice   ☐ Secuiryt   ☐ Quiet   ☐ Noisy

Our Rating: ☆ ☆ ☆ ☆ ☆
GPS: _____
Altitude: _____
Cell Service / Carrier: _____
☐ Antenna Reception   ☐ Satellite TV   ☐ Cable TV
☐ Wifi Available   ☐ Free ☐ Fee $_____
Memberships: _____
Ammenities: _____

Location	☺	😐	☹	Water Pressure	☺	😐	☹
Restrooms	☺	😐	☹	Laundry	☺	😐	☹
Pool	☺	😐	☹	Hot Tub	☺	😐	☹

Places Visited / Activities: _____
_____
_____

People Met / New Friends: _____
_____
_____

Food, Dining & Restaurants: _____
_____
_____

Highlights / Memorable Events: _____
_____
_____

Places To Go & Things To Do for Next Time: _____
_____
_____

NOTES:

Date: _____

Weather:

From: _____

To: _____

Route Taken: _____
_____

Beginning Mileage: _____

Ending Mileage: _____

Total Miles Traveled: _____

Campground Information

Name: _____

Address: _____

Phone: _____

Site # _____ $ _____ ☐ Day ☐ Week ☐ Month

☐ First Visit   ☐ Return Visit   ☐ Easy Access
☐ Site Level   ☐ Back-in   ☐ Pull-through
☐ 15 amp   ☐ 30 amp   ☐ 50 amp
☐ Water   ☐ Sewer   ☐ Shade   ☐ Sun
☐ Paved   ☐ Sand / Grass   ☐ Gravel
☐ Picnic Table   ☐ Fire ring   ☐ Trees   ☐ Lawn
☐ Patio   ☐ Kid Friendly   ☐ Pet Friendly
☐ Store   ☐ Cafe   ☐ Firewood
☐ Ice   ☐ Secuiryt   ☐ Quiet   ☐ Noisy

Our Rating: ☆ ☆ ☆ ☆ ☆

GPS: _____

Altitude: _____

Cell Service / Carrier: _____

☐ Antenna Reception   ☐ Satellite TV   ☐ Cable TV
☐ Wifi Available   ☐ Free ☐ Fee $ _____

Memberships: _____

Ammenities: _____

Location   ☺ ☹ ☹   Water Pressure   ☺ ☹ ☹
Restrooms   ☺ ☹ ☹   Laundry   ☺ ☹ ☹
Pool   ☺ ☹ ☹   Hot Tub   ☺ ☹ ☹

Places Visited / Activities: _____
_____
_____
_____
_____

People Met / New Friends: _____
_____
_____
_____
_____

Food, Dining & Restaurants: _____
_____
_____
_____
_____

Highlights / Memorable Events: _____
_____
_____
_____
_____

Places To Go & Things To Do for Next Time: _____
_____
_____
_____
_____

NOTES:

Date:	From:	Beginning Mileage:
Weather: ☀ ⛅ ☔ ❄ 🌡 🌡 🎏 ☁	To:	Ending Mileage:
	Route Taken:	Total Miles Traveled:

Campground Information

Name: _____

Address: _____

Phone: _____

Our Rating: ☆ ☆ ☆ ☆ ☆

GPS: _____

Altitude: _____

Site # _____ $ _____ ☐ Day ☐ Week ☐ Month

Cell Service / Carrier: _____

☐ First Visit ☐ Return Visit ☐ Easy Access
☐ Site Level ☐ Back-in   ☐ Pull-through
☐ 15 amp   ☐ 30 amp   ☐ 50 amp
☐ Water   ☐ Sewer   ☐ Shade   ☐ Sun
☐ Paved   ☐ Sand / Grass ☐ Gravel
☐ Picnic Table ☐ Fire ring   ☐ Trees   ☐ Lawn
☐ Patio   ☐ Kid Friendly ☐ Pet Friendly
☐ Store   ☐ Cafe   ☐ Firewood
☐ Ice   ☐ Secuiryt   ☐ Quiet   ☐ Noisy

☐ Antenna Reception ☐ Satellite TV ☐ Cable TV
☐ Wifi Available   ☐ Free ☐ Fee $_____

Memberships: _____

Ammenities: _____

Location	☺ ☺ ☹	Water Pressure	☺ ☺ ☹
Restrooms	☺ ☺ ☹	Laundry	☺ ☺ ☹
Pool	☺ ☺ ☹	Hot Tub	☺ ☺ ☹

Places Visited / Activities: _____

_____

_____

People Met / New Friends: _____

_____

_____

Food, Dining & Restaurants: _____

_____

_____

Highlights / Memorable Events: _____

_____

_____

Places To Go & Things To Do for Next Time: _____

_____

_____

Notes:

Date: _____
Weather:

From: _____
To: _____
Route Taken: _____
_____

Beginning Mileage: _____
Ending Mileage: _____
Total Miles Traveled: _____

Campground Information

Name: _____
Address: _____
Phone: _____

Our Rating: ☆ ☆ ☆ ☆ ☆
GPS: _____
Altitude: _____

Site # _____ $ _____ ☐ Day ☐ Week ☐ Month

☐ First Visit	☐ Return Visit	☐ Easy Access
☐ Site Level	☐ Back-in	☐ Pull-through
☐ 15 amp	☐ 30 amp	☐ 50 amp
☐ Water	☐ Sewer	☐ Shade ☐ Sun
☐ Paved	☐ Sand / Grass	☐ Gravel
☐ Picnic Table	☐ Fire ring	☐ Trees ☐ Lawn
☐ Patio	☐ Kid Friendly	☐ Pet Friendly
☐ Store	☐ Cafe	☐ Firewood
☐ Ice	☐ Secuiryt	☐ Quiet ☐ Noisy

Cell Service / Carrier: _____
☐ Antenna Reception ☐ Satellite TV ☐ Cable TV
☐ Wifi Available ☐ Free ☐ Fee $ _____
Memberships: _____
Ammenities: _____

	☺	😐	☹		☺	😐	☹
Location	☺	😐	☹	Water Pressure	☺	😐	☹
Restrooms	☺	😐	☹	Laundry	☺	😐	☹
Pool	☺	😐	☹	Hot Tub	☺	😐	☹

Places Visited / Activities: _____
_____
_____
_____

People Met / New Friends: _____
_____
_____
_____

Food, Dining & Restaurants: _____
_____
_____
_____

Highlights / Memorable Events: _____
_____
_____
_____

Places To Go & Things To Do for Next Time: _____
_____
_____
_____

NOTES:

Date: _____

Weather:

From: _____
To: _____
Route Taken: _____
_____

Beginning Mileage: _____
Ending Mileage: _____
Total Miles Traveled: _____

Campground Information

Name: _____
Address: _____
Phone: _____

Our Rating: ☆ ☆ ☆ ☆ ☆
GPS: _____
Altitude: _____

Site # _____ $ _____ ☐ Day ☐ Week ☐ Month

☐ First Visit   ☐ Return Visit   ☐ Easy Access
☐ Site Level   ☐ Back-in   ☐ Pull-through
☐ 15 amp   ☐ 30 amp   ☐ 50 amp
☐ Water   ☐ Sewer   ☐ Shade   ☐ Sun
☐ Paved   ☐ Sand / Grass   ☐ Gravel
☐ Picnic Table ☐ Fire ring   ☐ Trees   ☐ Lawn
☐ Patio   ☐ Kid Friendly   ☐ Pet Friendly
☐ Store   ☐ Cafe   ☐ Firewood
☐ Ice   ☐ Secuiryt   ☐ Quiet   ☐ Noisy

Cell Service / Carrier: _____
☐ Antenna Reception   ☐ Satellite TV   ☐ Cable TV
☐ Wifi Available   ☐ Free ☐ Fee $ _____
Memberships: _____
Ammenities: _____

Location	☺	😐	☹	Water Pressure	☺	😐	☹
Restrooms	☺	😐	☹	Laundry	☺	😐	☹
Pool	☺	😐	☹	Hot Tub	☺	😐	☹

Places Visited / Activities: _____
_____
_____
_____

People Met / New Friends: _____
_____
_____
_____

Food, Dining & Restaurants: _____
_____
_____
_____

Highlights / Memorable Events: _____
_____
_____
_____

Places To Go & Things To Do for Next Time: _____
_____
_____
_____

NOTES:

Date: _____	From: _____	Beginning Mileage: _____
Weather: ☀ ⛅ ☂ ❄ 🌡 🌡 📢 ☁	To: _____	Ending Mileage: _____
	Route Taken: _____	Total Miles Traveled: _____

Campground Information

Name: _____

Address: _____

Phone: _____

Our Rating: ☆ ☆ ☆ ☆ ☆

GPS: _____

Altitude: _____

Site # _____ $ _____ ☐ Day ☐ Week ☐ Month

Cell Service / Carrier: _____

☐ First Visit ☐ Return Visit ☐ Easy Access
☐ Site Level ☐ Back-in ☐ Pull-through
☐ 15 amp ☐ 30 amp ☐ 50 amp
☐ Water ☐ Sewer ☐ Shade ☐ Sun
☐ Paved ☐ Sand / Grass ☐ Gravel
☐ Picnic Table ☐ Fire ring ☐ Trees ☐ Lawn
☐ Patio ☐ Kid Friendly ☐ Pet Friendly
☐ Store ☐ Cafe ☐ Firewood
☐ Ice ☐ Secuiryt ☐ Quiet ☐ Noisy

☐ Antenna Reception ☐ Satellite TV ☐ Cable TV
☐ Wifi Available ☐ Free ☐ Fee $ _____

Memberships: _____

Ammenities: _____

Location	😊	😐	☹	Water Pressure	😊	😐	☹
Restrooms	😊	😐	☹	Laundry	😊	😐	☹
Pool	😊	😐	☹	Hot Tub	😊	😐	☹

Places Visited / Activities: _____

_____

_____

People Met / New Friends: _____

_____

_____

Food, Dining & Restaurants: _____

_____

_____

Highlights / Memorable Events: _____

_____

_____

Places To Go & Things To Do for Next Time: _____

_____

_____

NOTES:

Date: _____	From: _____	Beginning Mileage: _____
Weather: ☀ ⛅ ☔ ❄ 🌡 🌡 📢 ☁	To: _____ Route Taken: _____ _____	Ending Mileage: _____ Total Miles Traveled: _____

CAMPGROUND INFORMATION

Name: _____   Our Rating: ☆ ☆ ☆ ☆ ☆

Address: _____   GPS: _____

Phone: _____   Altitude: _____

Site # _____ $ _____ ☐ Day ☐ Week ☐ Month   Cell Service / Carrier: _____

☐ First Visit	☐ Return Visit	☐ Easy Access		☐ Antenna Reception	☐ Satellite TV	☐ Cable TV
☐ Site Level	☐ Back-in	☐ Pull-through		☐ Wifi Available	☐ Free ☐ Fee	$ _____
☐ 15 amp	☐ 30 amp	☐ 50 amp				
☐ Water	☐ Sewer	☐ Shade	☐ Sun	Memberships: _____		
☐ Paved	☐ Sand / Grass	☐ Gravel		Ammenities: _____		
☐ Picnic Table	☐ Fire ring	☐ Trees	☐ Lawn	Location ☺ 😐 ☹ Water Pressure ☺ 😐 ☹		
☐ Patio	☐ Kid Friendly	☐ Pet Friendly		Restrooms ☺ 😐 ☹ Laundry ☺ 😐 ☹		
☐ Store	☐ Cafe	☐ Firewood		Pool ☺ 😐 ☹ Hot Tub ☺ 😐 ☹		
☐ Ice	☐ Secuiryt	☐ Quiet	☐ Noisy			

PLACES VISITED / ACTIVITIES: _____

_____

_____

_____

PEOPLE MET / NEW FRIENDS: _____

_____

_____

_____

FOOD, DINING & RESTAURANTS: _____

_____

_____

_____

HIGHLIGHTS / MEMORABLE EVENTS: _____

_____

_____

_____

PLACES TO GO & THINGS TO DO FOR NEXT TIME: _____

_____

_____

_____

NOTES:

Date: _____ From: _____ Beginning Mileage: _____

Weather: ☀ ⛅ ☔ ❄ 🌡 🌡 🚩 ⛈ To: _____ Ending Mileage: _____

Route Taken: _____ Total Miles Traveled: _____

Campground Information

Name: _____

Address: _____

Phone: _____

Our Rating: ☆ ☆ ☆ ☆ ☆

GPS: _____

Altitude: _____

Site # _____ $ _____ ☐ Day ☐ Week ☐ Month

Cell Service / Carrier: _____

☐ First Visit	☐ Return Visit	☐ Easy Access
☐ Site Level	☐ Back-in	☐ Pull-through
☐ 15 amp	☐ 30 amp	☐ 50 amp
☐ Water	☐ Sewer	☐ Shade ☐ Sun
☐ Paved	☐ Sand / Grass	☐ Gravel
☐ Picnic Table	☐ Fire ring	☐ Trees ☐ Lawn
☐ Patio	☐ Kid Friendly	☐ Pet Friendly
☐ Store	☐ Cafe	☐ Firewood
☐ Ice	☐ Secuiryt	☐ Quiet ☐ Noisy

☐ Antenna Reception ☐ Satellite TV ☐ Cable TV
☐ Wifi Available ☐ Free ☐ Fee $_____

Memberships: _____

Ammenities: _____

Location ☺ 😐 ☹   Water Pressure ☺ 😐 ☹
Restrooms ☺ 😐 ☹   Laundry ☺ 😐 ☹
Pool ☺ 😐 ☹   Hot Tub ☺ 😐 ☹

Places Visited / Activities: _____

_____

_____

People Met / New Friends: _____

_____

_____

Food, Dining & Restaurants: _____

_____

_____

Highlights / Memorable Events: _____

_____

_____

Places To Go & Things To Do for Next Time: _____

_____

_____

NOTES:

Date: _____ From: _____ Beginning Mileage: _____

Weather: ☀ ⛅ ☔ ❄ 🌡 🌡 📯 ⛈

To: _____ Ending Mileage: _____

Route Taken: _____
_____ Total Miles Traveled: _____

Campground Information

Name: _____

Address: _____

Phone: _____

Site # _____ $ _____ ☐ Day ☐ Week ☐ Month

- ☐ First Visit
- ☐ Site Level
- ☐ 15 amp
- ☐ Water
- ☐ Paved
- ☐ Picnic Table
- ☐ Patio
- ☐ Store
- ☐ Ice

- ☐ Return Visit
- ☐ Back-in
- ☐ 30 amp
- ☐ Sewer
- ☐ Sand / Grass
- ☐ Fire ring
- ☐ Kid Friendly
- ☐ Cafe
- ☐ Secuiryt

- ☐ Easy Access
- ☐ Pull-through
- ☐ 50 amp
- ☐ Shade ☐ Sun
- ☐ Gravel
- ☐ Trees ☐ Lawn
- ☐ Pet Friendly
- ☐ Firewood
- ☐ Quiet ☐ Noisy

Our Rating: ☆ ☆ ☆ ☆ ☆

GPS: _____

Altitude: _____

Cell Service / Carrier: _____

- ☐ Antenna Reception ☐ Satellite TV ☐ Cable TV
- ☐ Wifi Available ☐ Free ☐ Fee $ _____

Memberships: _____

Ammenities: _____

	☺	😐	☹		☺	😐	☹
Location	☺	😐	☹	Water Pressure	☺	😐	☹
Restrooms	☺	😐	☹	Laundry	☺	😐	☹
Pool	☺	😐	☹	Hot Tub	☺	😐	☹

Places Visited / Activities:
_____
_____
_____
_____

People Met / New Friends:
_____
_____
_____
_____

Food, Dining & Restaurants:
_____
_____
_____
_____

Highlights / Memorable Events:
_____
_____
_____
_____

Places To Go & Things To Do for Next Time:
_____
_____
_____
_____

NOTES:

Date: _____	From: _____	Beginning Mileage: _____
Weather:	To: _____	Ending Mileage: _____
☀ ⛅ ☂ ❄ 🌡 🌡 📢 ☁	Route Taken: _____ _____	Total Miles Traveled: _____

Campground Information

Name: _____

Address: _____

Phone: _____

Site # _____ $ _____ ☐ Day ☐ Week ☐ Month

☐ First Visit ☐ Return Visit ☐ Easy Access
☐ Site Level ☐ Back-in ☐ Pull-through
☐ 15 amp ☐ 30 amp ☐ 50 amp
☐ Water ☐ Sewer ☐ Shade ☐ Sun
☐ Paved ☐ Sand / Grass ☐ Gravel
☐ Picnic Table ☐ Fire ring ☐ Trees ☐ Lawn
☐ Patio ☐ Kid Friendly ☐ Pet Friendly
☐ Store ☐ Cafe ☐ Firewood
☐ Ice ☐ Secuirty ☐ Quiet ☐ Noisy

Our Rating: ☆ ☆ ☆ ☆ ☆

GPS: _____

Altitude: _____

Cell Service / Carrier: _____

☐ Antenna Reception ☐ Satellite TV ☐ Cable TV
☐ Wifi Available ☐ Free ☐ Fee $_____

Memberships: _____

Ammenities: _____

Location	🙂	😐	☹	Water Pressure	🙂	😐	☹
Restrooms	🙂	😐	☹	Laundry	🙂	😐	☹
Pool	🙂	😐	☹	Hot Tub	🙂	😐	☹

Places Visited / Activities:
_____
_____
_____

People Met / New Friends:
_____
_____
_____

Food, Dining & Restaurants:
_____
_____
_____

Highlights / Memorable Events:
_____
_____
_____

Places To Go & Things To Do for Next Time:
_____
_____
_____

NOTES:

Date: _____ From: _____ Beginning Mileage: _____

Weather: To: _____ Ending Mileage: _____

Route Taken: _____

_____ Total Miles Traveled: _____

Campground Information

Name: _____ Our Rating: ☆ ☆ ☆ ☆ ☆

Address: _____ GPS: _____

Phone: _____ Altitude: _____

Site # _____ $ _____ ☐ Day ☐ Week ☐ Month Cell Service / Carrier: _____

☐ First Visit   ☐ Return Visit   ☐ Easy Access   ☐ Antenna Reception   ☐ Satellite TV   ☐ Cable TV
☐ Site Level   ☐ Back-in   ☐ Pull-through   ☐ Wifi Available   ☐ Free ☐ Fee $ _____
☐ 15 amp   ☐ 30 amp   ☐ 50 amp
☐ Water   ☐ Sewer   ☐ Shade ☐ Sun   Memberships: _____
☐ Paved   ☐ Sand / Grass   ☐ Gravel   Ammenities: _____
☐ Picnic Table ☐ Fire ring   ☐ Trees ☐ Lawn   Location ☺ ☺ ☹   Water Pressure ☺ ☺ ☹
☐ Patio   ☐ Kid Friendly   ☐ Pet Friendly   Restrooms ☺ ☺ ☹   Laundry   ☺ ☺ ☹
☐ Store   ☐ Cafe   ☐ Firewood   Pool   ☺ ☺ ☹   Hot Tub   ☺ ☺ ☹
☐ Ice   ☐ Secuiryt   ☐ Quiet ☐ Noisy

Places Visited / Activities: _____

_____
_____
_____

People Met / New Friends: _____

_____
_____
_____

Food, Dining & Restaurants: _____

_____
_____
_____

Highlights / Memorable Events: _____

_____
_____
_____

Places To Go & Things To Do for Next Time: _____

_____
_____
_____

NOTES:

Date: _____ From: _____ Beginning Mileage: _____

Weather: To: _____ Ending Mileage: _____

Route Taken: _____ Total Miles Traveled: _____

Campground Information

Name: _____ Our Rating: ☆ ☆ ☆ ☆ ☆

Address: _____ GPS: _____

Phone: _____ Altitude: _____

Site # _____ $ _____ ☐ Day ☐ Week ☐ Month Cell Service / Carrier: _____

☐ First Visit ☐ Return Visit ☐ Easy Access ☐ Antenna Reception ☐ Satellite TV ☐ Cable TV
☐ Site Level ☐ Back-in   ☐ Pull-through ☐ Wifi Available   ☐ Free ☐ Fee $_____
☐ 15 amp   ☐ 30 amp   ☐ 50 amp
☐ Water   ☐ Sewer   ☐ Shade ☐ Sun Memberships: _____
☐ Paved   ☐ Sand / Grass ☐ Gravel   Ammenities: _____
☐ Picnic Table ☐ Fire ring ☐ Trees ☐ Lawn Location   ☺ ☹ ☹   Water Pressure ☺ ☹ ☹
☐ Patio   ☐ Kid Friendly ☐ Pet Friendly   Restrooms   ☺ ☹ ☹   Laundry   ☺ ☹ ☹
☐ Store   ☐ Cafe   ☐ Firewood   Pool   ☺ ☹ ☹   Hot Tub   ☺ ☹ ☹
☐ Ice   ☐ Secuiryt   ☐ Quiet ☐ Noisy

Places Visited / Activities: _____

People Met / New Friends: _____

Food, Dining & Restaurants: _____

Highlights / Memorable Events: _____

Places To Go & Things To Do for Next Time: _____

NOTES:

Date: _____
Weather:

From: _____
To: _____
Route Taken: _____
_____

Beginning Mileage: _____
Ending Mileage: _____
Total Miles Traveled: _____

Campground Information

Name: _____
Address: _____
Phone: _____

Site # _____ $ _____ ☐ Day ☐ Week ☐ Month

☐ First Visit	☐ Return Visit	☐ Easy Access
☐ Site Level	☐ Back-in	☐ Pull-through
☐ 15 amp	☐ 30 amp	☐ 50 amp
☐ Water	☐ Sewer	☐ Shade ☐ Sun
☐ Paved	☐ Sand / Grass	☐ Gravel
☐ Picnic Table	☐ Fire ring	☐ Trees ☐ Lawn
☐ Patio	☐ Kid Friendly	☐ Pet Friendly
☐ Store	☐ Cafe	☐ Firewood
☐ Ice	☐ Secuiryt	☐ Quiet ☐ Noisy

Our Rating: ☆ ☆ ☆ ☆ ☆
GPS: _____
Altitude: _____
Cell Service / Carrier: _____
☐ Antenna Reception ☐ Satellite TV ☐ Cable TV
☐ Wifi Available ☐ Free ☐ Fee $ _____
Memberships: _____
Amenities: _____

Location	☺ ☹ ☹	Water Pressure	☺ ☹ ☹
Restrooms	☺ ☹ ☹	Laundry	☺ ☹ ☹
Pool	☺ ☹ ☹	Hot Tub	☺ ☹ ☹

Places Visited / Activities: _____
_____
_____
_____

People Met / New Friends: _____
_____
_____
_____

Food, Dining & Restaurants: _____
_____
_____
_____

Highlights / Memorable Events: _____
_____
_____
_____

Places To Go & Things To Do for Next Time: _____
_____
_____
_____

NOTES:

Date:	From:	Beginning Mileage:
Weather:	To:	Ending Mileage:
	Route Taken:	Total Miles Traveled:

Campground Information

Name: _____

Address: _____

Phone: _____

Site # _____ $ _____ ☐ Day ☐ Week ☐ Month

☐ First Visit ☐ Return Visit ☐ Easy Access
☐ Site Level ☐ Back-in ☐ Pull-through
☐ 15 amp ☐ 30 amp ☐ 50 amp
☐ Water ☐ Sewer ☐ Shade ☐ Sun
☐ Paved ☐ Sand / Grass ☐ Gravel
☐ Picnic Table ☐ Fire ring ☐ Trees ☐ Lawn
☐ Patio ☐ Kid Friendly ☐ Pet Friendly
☐ Store ☐ Cafe ☐ Firewood
☐ Ice ☐ Secuiryt ☐ Quiet ☐ Noisy

Our Rating: ☆ ☆ ☆ ☆ ☆

GPS: _____

Altitude: _____

Cell Service / Carrier: _____

☐ Antenna Reception ☐ Satellite TV ☐ Cable TV
☐ Wifi Available ☐ Free ☐ Fee $_____

Memberships: _____

Ammenities: _____

Location	☺	😐	☹	Water Pressure	☺	😐	☹
Restrooms	☺	😐	☹	Laundry	☺	😐	☹
Pool	☺	😐	☹	Hot Tub	☺	😐	☹

Places Visited / Activities: _____

_____

_____

_____

People Met / New Friends: _____

_____

_____

_____

Food, Dining & Restaurants: _____

_____

_____

_____

Highlights / Memorable Events: _____

_____

_____

_____

Places To Go & Things To Do for Next Time: _____

_____

_____

_____

NOTES:

| Date: _____ | From: _____ | Beginning Mileage: _____ |
| Weather: ☀ ⛅ ☔ ❄ 🌡 🌡 📢 🌫 | To: _____
Route Taken: _____
_____ | Ending Mileage: _____
Total Miles Traveled: _____ |

Campground Information

Name: _____
Address: _____
Phone: _____

Site # _____ $ _____ ☐ Day ☐ Week ☐ Month

☐ First Visit ☐ Return Visit ☐ Easy Access
☐ Site Level ☐ Back-in ☐ Pull-through
☐ 15 amp ☐ 30 amp ☐ 50 amp
☐ Water ☐ Sewer ☐ Shade ☐ Sun
☐ Paved ☐ Sand / Grass ☐ Gravel
☐ Picnic Table ☐ Fire ring ☐ Trees ☐ Lawn
☐ Patio ☐ Kid Friendly ☐ Pet Friendly
☐ Store ☐ Cafe ☐ Firewood
☐ Ice ☐ Secuiryt ☐ Quiet ☐ Noisy

Our Rating: ☆ ☆ ☆ ☆ ☆
GPS: _____
Altitude: _____
Cell Service / Carrier: _____
☐ Antenna Reception ☐ Satellite TV ☐ Cable TV
☐ Wifi Available ☐ Free ☐ Fee $ _____
Memberships: _____
Ammenities: _____

Location	☺ 😐 ☹	Water Pressure	☺ 😐 ☹
Restrooms	☺ 😐 ☹	Laundry	☺ 😐 ☹
Pool	☺ 😐 ☹	Hot Tub	☺ 😐 ☹

PLACES VISITED / ACTIVITIES: _____
_____
_____
_____

PEOPLE MET / NEW FRIENDS: _____
_____
_____
_____

FOOD, DINING & RESTAURANTS: _____
_____
_____
_____

HIGHLIGHTS / MEMORABLE EVENTS: _____
_____
_____
_____

PLACES TO GO & THINGS TO DO FOR NEXT TIME: _____
_____
_____
_____

NOTES:

Date: _____

Weather:
☀ ⛅ ☂ ❄
🌡 🌡 🚩 ☁

From: _____
To: _____
Route Taken: _____
_____

Beginning Mileage: _____

Ending Mileage: _____

Total Miles Traveled: _____

Campground Information

Name: _____
Address: _____
Phone: _____

Site # _____ $ _____ ☐ Day ☐ Week ☐ Month
- ☐ First Visit
- ☐ Site Level
- ☐ 15 amp
- ☐ Water
- ☐ Paved
- ☐ Picnic Table
- ☐ Patio
- ☐ Store
- ☐ Ice

- ☐ Return Visit
- ☐ Back-in
- ☐ 30 amp
- ☐ Sewer
- ☐ Sand / Grass
- ☐ Fire ring
- ☐ Kid Friendly
- ☐ Cafe
- ☐ Secuiryt

- ☐ Easy Access
- ☐ Pull-through
- ☐ 50 amp
- ☐ Shade ☐ Sun
- ☐ Gravel
- ☐ Trees ☐ Lawn
- ☐ Pet Friendly
- ☐ Firewood
- ☐ Quiet ☐ Noisy

Our Rating: ☆ ☆ ☆ ☆ ☆

GPS: _____
Altitude: _____
Cell Service / Carrier: _____

- ☐ Antenna Reception
- ☐ Wifi Available

- ☐ Satellite TV
- ☐ Free ☐ Fee $_____

- ☐ Cable TV

Memberships: _____
Ammenities: _____

Location	☺	😐	☹	Water Pressure	☺	😐	☹
Restrooms	☺	😐	☹	Laundry	☺	😐	☹
Pool	☺	😐	☹	Hot Tub	☺	😐	☹

Places Visited / Activities: _____
_____
_____
_____

People Met / New Friends: _____
_____
_____
_____

Food, Dining & Restaurants: _____
_____
_____
_____

Highlights / Memorable Events: _____
_____
_____
_____

Places To Go & Things To Do for Next Time: _____
_____
_____
_____

NOTES:

| Date: _____ | From: _____ | Beginning Mileage: _____ |
| Weather: ☀ ⛅ ☔ ❄ 🌡🔥 🌡❄ 📢 ☁ | To: _____
Route Taken: _____
_____ | Ending Mileage: _____

Total Miles Traveled: _____ |

Campground Information

Name: _____
Address: _____
Phone: _____

Site # _____ $ _____ ☐ Day ☐ Week ☐ Month

☐ First Visit ☐ Return Visit ☐ Easy Access
☐ Site Level ☐ Back-in ☐ Pull-through
☐ 15 amp ☐ 30 amp ☐ 50 amp
☐ Water ☐ Sewer ☐ Shade ☐ Sun
☐ Paved ☐ Sand / Grass ☐ Gravel
☐ Picnic Table ☐ Fire ring ☐ Trees ☐ Lawn
☐ Patio ☐ Kid Friendly ☐ Pet Friendly
☐ Store ☐ Cafe ☐ Firewood
☐ Ice ☐ Secuiryt ☐ Quiet ☐ Noisy

Our Rating: ☆ ☆ ☆ ☆ ☆
GPS: _____
Altitude: _____
Cell Service / Carrier: _____

☐ Antenna Reception ☐ Satellite TV ☐ Cable TV
☐ Wifi Available ☐ Free ☐ Fee $_____

Memberships: _____
Ammenities: _____

	☺ 😐 ☹		☺ 😐 ☹
Location	☺ 😐 ☹	Water Pressure	☺ 😐 ☹
Restrooms	☺ 😐 ☹	Laundry	☺ 😐 ☹
Pool	☺ 😐 ☹	Hot Tub	☺ 😐 ☹

Places Visited / Activities:
_____
_____
_____
_____

People Met / New Friends:
_____
_____
_____
_____

Food, Dining & Restaurants:
_____
_____
_____
_____

Highlights / Memorable Events:
_____
_____
_____
_____

Places To Go & Things To Do for Next Time:
_____
_____
_____
_____

NOTES:

Date: _____ From: _____ Beginning Mileage: _____

Weather: To: _____ Ending Mileage: _____

Route Taken: _____

_____ Total Miles Traveled: _____

Campground Information

Name: _____ Our Rating: ☆ ☆ ☆ ☆ ☆

Address: _____ GPS: _____

Phone: _____ Altitude: _____

Site # _____ $ _____ ☐ Day ☐ Week ☐ Month Cell Service / Carrier: _____

☐ First Visit	☐ Return Visit	☐ Easy Access	☐ Antenna Reception ☐ Satellite TV ☐ Cable TV
☐ Site Level	☐ Back-in	☐ Pull-through	☐ Wifi Available ☐ Free ☐ Fee $_____
☐ 15 amp	☐ 30 amp	☐ 50 amp	
☐ Water	☐ Sewer	☐ Shade ☐ Sun	Memberships: _____
☐ Paved	☐ Sand / Grass	☐ Gravel	Ammenities: _____
☐ Picnic Table	☐ Fire ring	☐ Trees ☐ Lawn	Location ☺ 😐 ☹ Water Pressure ☺ 😐 ☹
☐ Patio	☐ Kid Friendly	☐ Pet Friendly	Restrooms ☺ 😐 ☹ Laundry ☺ 😐 ☹
☐ Store	☐ Cafe	☐ Firewood	Pool ☺ 😐 ☹ Hot Tub ☺ 😐 ☹
☐ Ice	☐ Secuiryt	☐ Quiet ☐ Noisy	

Places Visited / Activities: _____

_____

_____

_____

People Met / New Friends: _____

_____

_____

_____

Food, Dining & Restaurants: _____

_____

_____

_____

Highlights / Memorable Events: _____

_____

_____

_____

Places To Go & Things To Do for Next Time: _____

_____

_____

_____

Notes:

Date: _____   From: _____   Beginning Mileage: _____

Weather: To: _____   Ending Mileage: _____

                          Route Taken: _____
                          _____   Total Miles Traveled: _____

Campground Information

Name: _____   Our Rating: ☆ ☆ ☆ ☆ ☆

Address: _____   GPS: _____

Phone: _____   Altitude: _____

Site # _____ $ _____ ☐ Day ☐ Week ☐ Month   Cell Service / Carrier: _____

☐ First Visit	☐ Return Visit	☐ Easy Access
☐ Site Level	☐ Back-in	☐ Pull-through
☐ 15 amp	☐ 30 amp	☐ 50 amp
☐ Water	☐ Sewer	☐ Shade ☐ Sun
☐ Paved	☐ Sand / Grass	☐ Gravel
☐ Picnic Table	☐ Fire ring	☐ Trees ☐ Lawn
☐ Patio	☐ Kid Friendly	☐ Pet Friendly
☐ Store	☐ Cafe	☐ Firewood
☐ Ice	☐ Secuiryt	☐ Quiet ☐ Noisy

☐ Antenna Reception   ☐ Satellite TV   ☐ Cable TV
☐ Wifi Available   ☐ Free ☐ Fee $ _____

Memberships: _____

Ammenities: _____

Location   ☺ 😐 ☹   Water Pressure   ☺ 😐 ☹
Restrooms   ☺ 😐 ☹   Laundry   ☺ 😐 ☹
Pool   ☺ 😐 ☹   Hot Tub   ☺ 😐 ☹

Places Visited / Activities: _____

_____
_____
_____

People Met / New Friends: _____

_____
_____
_____

Food, Dining & Restaurants: _____

_____
_____
_____

Highlights / Memorable Events: _____

_____
_____
_____

Places To Go & Things To Do for Next Time: _____

_____
_____
_____

Notes:

Date: _____ From: _____ Beginning Mileage: _____

Weather: To: _____ Ending Mileage: _____

Route Taken: _____ Total Miles Traveled: _____

Campground Information

Name: _____ Our Rating: ☆ ☆ ☆ ☆ ☆

Address: _____ GPS: _____

Phone: _____ Altitude: _____

Site #_____ $_____ ☐ Day ☐ Week ☐ Month Cell Service / Carrier: _____

☐ First Visit   ☐ Return Visit   ☐ Easy Access   ☐ Antenna Reception   ☐ Satellite TV   ☐ Cable TV
☐ Site Level   ☐ Back-in   ☐ Pull-through   ☐ Wifi Available   ☐ Free ☐ Fee $_____
☐ 15 amp   ☐ 30 amp   ☐ 50 amp
☐ Water   ☐ Sewer   ☐ Shade   ☐ Sun   Memberships: _____
☐ Paved   ☐ Sand / Grass   ☐ Gravel   Ammenities: _____
☐ Picnic Table   ☐ Fire ring   ☐ Trees   ☐ Lawn   Location   ☺ 😐 ☹   Water Pressure ☺ 😐 ☹
☐ Patio   ☐ Kid Friendly   ☐ Pet Friendly   Restrooms   ☺ 😐 ☹   Laundry   ☺ 😐 ☹
☐ Store   ☐ Cafe   ☐ Firewood   Pool   ☺ 😐 ☹   Hot Tub   ☺ 😐 ☹
☐ Ice   ☐ Secuiryt   ☐ Quiet   ☐ Noisy

Places Visited / Activities: _____

_____
_____
_____

People Met / New Friends: _____

_____
_____
_____

Food, Dining & Restaurants: _____

_____
_____
_____

Highlights / Memorable Events: _____

_____
_____
_____

Places To Go & Things To Do for Next Time: _____

_____
_____
_____

NOTES:

Date: _____ From: _____ Beginning Mileage: _____

Weather: To: _____ Ending Mileage: _____

Route Taken: _____

_____ Total Miles Traveled: _____

Campground Information

Name: _____ Our Rating: ☆ ☆ ☆ ☆

Address: _____ GPS: _____

Phone: _____ Altitude: _____

Site # _____ $ _____ ☐ Day ☐ Week ☐ Month Cell Service / Carrier: _____

☐ First Visit	☐ Return Visit	☐ Easy Access	☐ Antenna Reception ☐ Satellite TV ☐ Cable TV
☐ Site Level	☐ Back-in	☐ Pull-through	☐ Wifi Available ☐ Free ☐ Fee $_____
☐ 15 amp	☐ 30 amp	☐ 50 amp	Memberships: _____
☐ Water	☐ Sewer	☐ Shade ☐ Sun	Amenities: _____
☐ Paved	☐ Sand / Grass	☐ Gravel	
☐ Picnic Table	☐ Fire ring	☐ Trees ☐ Lawn	Location ☺ ☹ ☹ Water Pressure ☺ ☹ ☹
☐ Patio	☐ Kid Friendly	☐ Pet Friendly	Restrooms ☺ ☹ ☹ Laundry ☺ ☹ ☹
☐ Store	☐ Cafe	☐ Firewood	Pool ☺ ☹ ☹ Hot Tub ☺ ☹ ☹
☐ Ice	☐ Secuiryt	☐ Quiet ☐ Noisy	

Places Visited / Activities: _____

_____

_____

_____

People Met / New Friends: _____

_____

_____

_____

Food, Dining & Restaurants: _____

_____

_____

_____

Highlights / Memorable Events: _____

_____

_____

_____

Places To Go & Things To Do for Next Time: _____

_____

_____

_____

NOTES:

Date: _____

From: _____

To: _____

Route Taken: _____
_____

Weather:

Beginning Mileage: _____

Ending Mileage: _____

Total Miles Traveled: _____

Campground Information

Name: _____

Address: _____

Phone: _____

Site # _____ $ _____ ☐ Day ☐ Week ☐ Month

☐ First Visit ☐ Return Visit ☐ Easy Access
☐ Site Level ☐ Back-in ☐ Pull-through
☐ 15 amp ☐ 30 amp ☐ 50 amp
☐ Water ☐ Sewer ☐ Shade ☐ Sun
☐ Paved ☐ Sand / Grass ☐ Gravel
☐ Picnic Table ☐ Fire ring ☐ Trees ☐ Lawn
☐ Patio ☐ Kid Friendly ☐ Pet Friendly
☐ Store ☐ Cafe ☐ Firewood
☐ Ice ☐ Secuiryt ☐ Quiet ☐ Noisy

Our Rating: ☆ ☆ ☆ ☆ ☆

GPS: _____

Altitude: _____

Cell Service / Carrier: _____

☐ Antenna Reception ☐ Satellite TV ☐ Cable TV
☐ Wifi Available ☐ Free ☐ Fee $_____

Memberships: _____

Ammenities: _____

Location ☺ 😐 ☹ Water Pressure ☺ 😐 ☹
Restrooms ☺ 😐 ☹ Laundry ☺ 😐 ☹
Pool ☺ 😐 ☹ Hot Tub ☺ 😐 ☹

Places Visited / Activities: _____
_____
_____
_____

People Met / New Friends: _____
_____
_____
_____

Food, Dining & Restaurants: _____
_____
_____
_____

Highlights / Memorable Events: _____
_____
_____
_____

Places To Go & Things To Do for Next Time: _____
_____
_____
_____

NOTES:

Date: _____ From: _____ Beginning Mileage: _____

Weather: ☀ ⛅ ☂ ❄ To: _____ Ending Mileage: _____

🌡 🌡 🚩 ☁ Route Taken: _____

_____ Total Miles Traveled: _____

Campground Information

Name: _____ Our Rating: ☆ ☆ ☆ ☆ ☆

Address: _____ GPS: _____

Phone: _____ Altitude: _____

Site # _____ $ _____ ☐ Day ☐ Week ☐ Month Cell Service / Carrier: _____

☐ First Visit   ☐ Return Visit   ☐ Easy Access   ☐ Antenna Reception   ☐ Satellite TV   ☐ Cable TV
☐ Site Level   ☐ Back-in   ☐ Pull-through ☐ Wifi Available   ☐ Free ☐ Fee $_____
☐ 15 amp   ☐ 30 amp   ☐ 50 amp
☐ Water   ☐ Sewer   ☐ Shade ☐ Sun   Memberships: _____
☐ Paved   ☐ Sand / Grass   ☐ Gravel   Ammenities: _____
☐ Picnic Table ☐ Fire ring   ☐ Trees ☐ Lawn   Location   ☺ 😐 ☹   Water Pressure ☺ 😐 ☹
☐ Patio   ☐ Kid Friendly   ☐ Pet Friendly   Restrooms   ☺ 😐 ☹   Laundry   ☺ 😐 ☹
☐ Store   ☐ Cafe   ☐ Firewood   Pool   ☺ 😐 ☹   Hot Tub   ☺ 😐 ☹
☐ Ice   ☐ Secuiryt   ☐ Quiet ☐ Noisy

Places Visited / Activities: _____

_____

_____

People Met / New Friends: _____

_____

_____

Food, Dining & Restaurants: _____

_____

_____

Highlights / Memorable Events: _____

_____

_____

Places To Go & Things To Do for Next Time: _____

_____

_____

Notes:

Date: _____   From: _____   Beginning Mileage: _____

Weather: ☀ ⛅ ☂ ❄   To: _____   Ending Mileage: _____

🌡 🌡 🚩 🌧   Route Taken: _____
_____   Total Miles Traveled: _____

Campground Information

Name: _____   Our Rating: ☆ ☆ ☆ ☆ ☆

Address: _____   GPS: _____

Phone: _____   Altitude: _____

Site # _____ $ _____   ☐ Day ☐ Week ☐ Month   Cell Service / Carrier: _____

☐ First Visit   ☐ Return Visit   ☐ Easy Access   ☐ Antenna Reception   ☐ Satellite TV   ☐ Cable TV
☐ Site Level   ☐ Back-in   ☐ Pull-through   ☐ Wifi Available   ☐ Free ☐ Fee $ _____
☐ 15 amp   ☐ 30 amp   ☐ 50 amp
☐ Water   ☐ Sewer   ☐ Shade ☐ Sun   Memberships: _____
☐ Paved   ☐ Sand / Grass   ☐ Gravel   Ammenities: _____
☐ Picnic Table   ☐ Fire ring   ☐ Trees ☐ Lawn   Location   ☺ 😐 ☹   Water Pressure ☺ 😐 ☹
☐ Patio   ☐ Kid Friendly   ☐ Pet Friendly   Restrooms   ☺ 😐 ☹   Laundry   ☺ 😐 ☹
☐ Store   ☐ Cafe   ☐ Firewood   Pool   ☺ 😐 ☹   Hot Tub   ☺ 😐 ☹
☐ Ice   ☐ Secuiryt   ☐ Quiet ☐ Noisy

Places Visited / Activities: _____
_____
_____
_____
_____

People Met / New Friends: _____
_____
_____
_____
_____

Food, Dining & Restaurants: _____
_____
_____
_____
_____

Highlights / Memorable Events: _____
_____
_____
_____
_____

Places To Go & Things To Do for Next Time: _____
_____
_____
_____
_____

NOTES:

Date: _____
Weather:

From: _____
To: _____
Route Taken: _____
_____

Beginning Mileage: _____

Ending Mileage: _____

Total Miles Traveled: _____

Campground Information

Name: _____
Address: _____
Phone: _____

Site #_____ $_____ ☐ Day ☐ Week ☐ Month

☐ First Visit	☐ Return Visit	☐ Easy Access
☐ Site Level	☐ Back-in	☐ Pull-through
☐ 15 amp	☐ 30 amp	☐ 50 amp
☐ Water	☐ Sewer	☐ Shade ☐ Sun
☐ Paved	☐ Sand / Grass	☐ Gravel
☐ Picnic Table	☐ Fire ring	☐ Trees ☐ Lawn
☐ Patio	☐ Kid Friendly	☐ Pet Friendly
☐ Store	☐ Cafe	☐ Firewood
☐ Ice	☐ Secuiryt	☐ Quiet ☐ Noisy

Our Rating: ☆ ☆ ☆ ☆ ☆
GPS: _____
Altitude: _____
Cell Service / Carrier: _____

☐ Antenna Reception   ☐ Satellite TV   ☐ Cable TV
☐ Wifi Available   ☐ Free ☐ Fee $_____

Memberships: _____
Ammenities: _____

	☺	😐	☹		☺	😐	☹
Location	☺	😐	☹	Water Pressure	☺	😐	☹
Restrooms	☺	😐	☹	Laundry	☺	😐	☹
Pool	☺	😐	☹	Hot Tub	☺	😐	☹

Places Visited / Activities: _____
_____
_____
_____

People Met / New Friends: _____
_____
_____
_____

Food, Dining & Restaurants: _____
_____
_____
_____

Highlights / Memorable Events: _____
_____
_____
_____

Places To Go & Things To Do for Next Time: _____
_____
_____
_____

NOTES:

Date: _____   From: _____   Beginning Mileage: _____

Weather: To: _____   Ending Mileage: _____

                         Route Taken: _____
                         _____   Total Miles Traveled: _____

CAMPGROUND INFORMATION

Name: _____   Our Rating: ☆ ☆ ☆ ☆ ☆

Address: _____   GPS: _____

Phone: _____   Altitude: _____

Site # _____ $ _____ ☐ Day ☐ Week ☐ Month   Cell Service / Carrier: _____

☐ First Visit	☐ Return Visit	☐ Easy Access	☐ Antenna Reception	☐ Satellite TV	☐ Cable TV
☐ Site Level	☐ Back-in	☐ Pull-through	☐ Wifi Available	☐ Free ☐ Fee	$ _____
☐ 15 amp	☐ 30 amp	☐ 50 amp			
☐ Water	☐ Sewer	☐ Shade ☐ Sun	Memberships: _____		
☐ Paved	☐ Sand / Grass	☐ Gravel	Amenities: _____		
☐ Picnic Table	☐ Fire ring	☐ Trees ☐ Lawn	Location ☺ 😐 ☹	Water Pressure	☺ 😐 ☹
☐ Patio	☐ Kid Friendly	☐ Pet Friendly	Restrooms ☺ 😐 ☹	Laundry	☺ 😐 ☹
☐ Store	☐ Cafe	☐ Firewood	Pool ☺ 😐 ☹	Hot Tub	☺ 😐 ☹
☐ Ice	☐ Secuiryt	☐ Quiet ☐ Noisy			

PLACES VISITED / ACTIVITIES: _____
_____
_____
_____

PEOPLE MET / NEW FRIENDS: _____
_____
_____
_____

FOOD, DINING & RESTAURANTS: _____
_____
_____
_____

HIGHLIGHTS / MEMORABLE EVENTS: _____
_____
_____
_____

PLACES TO GO & THINGS TO DO FOR NEXT TIME: _____
_____
_____
_____

NOTES:

Date: _____	From: _____	Beginning Mileage: _____
Weather:	To: _____	Ending Mileage: _____
	Route Taken: _____	Total Miles Traveled: _____

Campground Information

Name: _____
Address: _____
Phone: _____

Site # _____ $ _____ ☐ Day ☐ Week ☐ Month

☐ First Visit   ☐ Return Visit   ☐ Easy Access
☐ Site Level   ☐ Back-in   ☐ Pull-through
☐ 15 amp   ☐ 30 amp   ☐ 50 amp
☐ Water   ☐ Sewer   ☐ Shade   ☐ Sun
☐ Paved   ☐ Sand / Grass   ☐ Gravel
☐ Picnic Table   ☐ Fire ring   ☐ Trees   ☐ Lawn
☐ Patio   ☐ Kid Friendly   ☐ Pet Friendly
☐ Store   ☐ Cafe   ☐ Firewood
☐ Ice   ☐ Secuiryt   ☐ Quiet   ☐ Noisy

Our Rating: ☆ ☆ ☆ ☆ ☆
GPS: _____
Altitude: _____
Cell Service / Carrier: _____

☐ Antenna Reception   ☐ Satellite TV   ☐ Cable TV
☐ Wifi Available   ☐ Free ☐ Fee $_____

Memberships: _____
Amenities: _____

Location	☺ ☺ ☹	Water Pressure	☺ ☺ ☹
Restrooms	☺ ☺ ☹	Laundry	☺ ☺ ☹
Pool	☺ ☺ ☹	Hot Tub	☺ ☺ ☹

Places Visited / Activities: _____

People Met / New Friends: _____

Food, Dining & Restaurants: _____

Highlights / Memorable Events: _____

Places To Go & Things To Do for Next Time: _____

Notes:

Date: _____ From: _____ Beginning Mileage: _____
Weather: To: _____ Ending Mileage: _____
  Route Taken: _____ Total Miles Traveled: _____

Campground Information

Name: _____ Our Rating: ☆ ☆ ☆ ☆ ☆
Address: _____ GPS: _____
Phone: _____ Altitude: _____

Site # _____ $ _____ ☐ Day ☐ Week ☐ Month Cell Service / Carrier: _____
☐ First Visit   ☐ Return Visit   ☐ Easy Access   ☐ Antenna Reception   ☐ Satellite TV   ☐ Cable TV
☐ Site Level   ☐ Back-in   ☐ Pull-through   ☐ Wifi Available   ☐ Free ☐ Fee $ _____
☐ 15 amp   ☐ 30 amp   ☐ 50 amp
☐ Water   ☐ Sewer   ☐ Shade ☐ Sun   Memberships: _____
☐ Paved   ☐ Sand / Grass   ☐ Gravel   Ammenities: _____
☐ Picnic Table ☐ Fire ring   ☐ Trees ☐ Lawn Location   ☺ 😐 ☹   Water Pressure ☺ 😐 ☹
☐ Patio   ☐ Kid Friendly   ☐ Pet Friendly   Restrooms   ☺ 😐 ☹   Laundry   ☺ 😐 ☹
☐ Store   ☐ Cafe   ☐ Firewood   Pool   ☺ 😐 ☹   Hot Tub   ☺ 😐 ☹
☐ Ice   ☐ Secuiryt   ☐ Quiet ☐ Noisy

Places Visited / Activities: _____

_____
_____

People Met / New Friends: _____

_____
_____

Food, Dining & Restaurants: _____

_____
_____

Highlights / Memorable Events: _____

_____
_____

Places To Go & Things To Do for Next Time: _____

_____
_____

Notes:

Date: _____   From: _____   Beginning Mileage: _____

Weather: To: _____   Ending Mileage: _____

                          Route Taken: _____   Total Miles Traveled: _____
                          _____

Campground Information

Name: _____   Our Rating: ☆ ☆ ☆ ☆ ☆

Address: _____   GPS: _____

Phone: _____   Altitude: _____

Site # _____ $ _____ ☐ Day ☐ Week ☐ Month   Cell Service / Carrier: _____

☐ First Visit   ☐ Return Visit   ☐ Easy Access   ☐ Antenna Reception   ☐ Satellite TV   ☐ Cable TV
☐ Site Level   ☐ Back-in   ☐ Pull-through   ☐ Wifi Available   ☐ Free ☐ Fee $_____
☐ 15 amp   ☐ 30 amp   ☐ 50 amp
☐ Water   ☐ Sewer   ☐ Shade   ☐ Sun   Memberships: _____
☐ Paved   ☐ Sand / Grass   ☐ Gravel   Ammenities: _____
☐ Picnic Table   ☐ Fire ring   ☐ Trees   ☐ Lawn Location   ☺ ☹ ☹   Water Pressure   ☺ ☹ ☹
☐ Patio   ☐ Kid Friendly   ☐ Pet Friendly   Restrooms ☺ ☹ ☹   Laundry   ☺ ☹ ☹
☐ Store   ☐ Cafe   ☐ Firewood   Pool   ☺ ☹ ☹   Hot Tub   ☺ ☹ ☹
☐ Ice   ☐ Secuiryt   ☐ Quiet   ☐ Noisy

Places Visited / Activities: _____
_____
_____

People Met / New Friends: _____
_____
_____

Food, Dining & Restaurants: _____
_____
_____

Highlights / Memorable Events: _____
_____
_____

Places To Go & Things To Do for Next Time: _____
_____
_____

NOTES:

Date: _____

From: _____

To: _____

Route Taken: _____

_____

Weather:

Beginning Mileage: _____

Ending Mileage: _____

Total Miles Traveled: _____

Campground Information

Name: _____

Address: _____

Phone: _____

Site # _____ $ _____ ☐ Day ☐ Week ☐ Month

☐ First Visit   ☐ Return Visit   ☐ Easy Access
☐ Site Level   ☐ Back-in   ☐ Pull-through
☐ 15 amp   ☐ 30 amp   ☐ 50 amp
☐ Water   ☐ Sewer   ☐ Shade   ☐ Sun
☐ Paved   ☐ Sand / Grass   ☐ Gravel
☐ Picnic Table   ☐ Fire ring   ☐ Trees   ☐ Lawn
☐ Patio   ☐ Kid Friendly   ☐ Pet Friendly
☐ Store   ☐ Cafe   ☐ Firewood
☐ Ice   ☐ Secuiryt   ☐ Quiet   ☐ Noisy

Our Rating: ☆ ☆ ☆ ☆ ☆

GPS: _____

Altitude: _____

Cell Service / Carrier: _____

☐ Antenna Reception   ☐ Satellite TV   ☐ Cable TV
☐ Wifi Available   ☐ Free   ☐ Fee $_____

Memberships: _____

Ammenities: _____

Location   ☺ 😐 ☹   Water Pressure ☺ 😐 ☹
Restrooms   ☺ 😐 ☹   Laundry   ☺ 😐 ☹
Pool   ☺ 😐 ☹   Hot Tub   ☺ 😐 ☹

Places Visited / Activities: _____

_____

_____

_____

People Met / New Friends: _____

_____

_____

_____

Food, Dining & Restaurants: _____

_____

_____

_____

Highlights / Memorable Events: _____

_____

_____

_____

Places To Go & Things To Do for Next Time: _____

_____

_____

_____

NOTES:

Date: _____   From: _____   Beginning Mileage: _____

Weather: To: _____   Ending Mileage: _____

                         Route Taken: _____
                         _____   Total Miles Traveled: _____

Campground Information

Name: _____   Our Rating: ☆ ☆ ☆ ☆ ☆

Address: _____   GPS: _____

Phone: _____   Altitude: _____

Site # _____ $ _____ ☐ Day ☐ Week ☐ Month   Cell Service / Carrier: _____

☐ First Visit   ☐ Return Visit   ☐ Easy Access   ☐ Antenna Reception   ☐ Satellite TV   ☐ Cable TV
☐ Site Level   ☐ Back-in   ☐ Pull-through   ☐ Wifi Available   ☐ Free ☐ Fee $ _____
☐ 15 amp   ☐ 30 amp   ☐ 50 amp
☐ Water   ☐ Sewer   ☐ Shade ☐ Sun   Memberships: _____
☐ Paved   ☐ Sand / Grass   ☐ Gravel   Ammenities: _____
☐ Picnic Table   ☐ Fire ring   ☐ Trees ☐ Lawn   Location   ☺ 😐 ☹   Water Pressure ☺ 😐 ☹
☐ Patio   ☐ Kid Friendly   ☐ Pet Friendly   Restrooms   ☺ 😐 ☹   Laundry   ☺ 😐 ☹
☐ Store   ☐ Cafe   ☐ Firewood   Pool   ☺ 😐 ☹   Hot Tub   ☺ 😐 ☹
☐ Ice   ☐ Secuiryt   ☐ Quiet ☐ Noisy

Places Visited / Activities: _____

_____
_____
_____

People Met / New Friends: _____

_____
_____
_____

Food, Dining & Restaurants: _____

_____
_____
_____

Highlights / Memorable Events: _____

_____
_____
_____

Places To Go & Things To Do for Next Time: _____

_____
_____
_____

Notes:

Date: _____
From: _____
Weather:
To: _____
Route Taken: _____
_____

Beginning Mileage: _____

Ending Mileage: _____

Total Miles Traveled: _____

CAMPGROUND INFORMATION

Name: _____
Address: _____
Phone: _____

Site # _____ $ _____ ☐ Day ☐ Week ☐ Month

☐ First Visit	☐ Return Visit	☐ Easy Access
☐ Site Level	☐ Back-in	☐ Pull-through
☐ 15 amp	☐ 30 amp	☐ 50 amp
☐ Water	☐ Sewer	☐ Shade ☐ Sun
☐ Paved	☐ Sand / Grass	☐ Gravel
☐ Picnic Table	☐ Fire ring	☐ Trees ☐ Lawn
☐ Patio	☐ Kid Friendly	☐ Pet Friendly
☐ Store	☐ Cafe	☐ Firewood
☐ Ice	☐ Secuiryt	☐ Quiet ☐ Noisy

Our Rating: ☆ ☆ ☆ ☆ ☆
GPS: _____
Altitude: _____
Cell Service / Carrier: _____

☐ Antenna Reception   ☐ Satellite TV   ☐ Cable TV
☐ Wifi Available   ☐ Free ☐ Fee $_____

Memberships: _____
Amenities: _____

Location	☺ ☺ ☹	Water Pressure	☺ ☺ ☹
Restrooms	☺ ☺ ☹	Laundry	☺ ☺ ☹
Pool	☺ ☺ ☹	Hot Tub	☺ ☺ ☹

PLACES VISITED / ACTIVITIES: _____
_____
_____
_____

PEOPLE MET / NEW FRIENDS: _____
_____
_____
_____

FOOD, DINING & RESTAURANTS: _____
_____
_____
_____

HIGHLIGHTS / MEMORABLE EVENTS: _____
_____
_____
_____

PLACES TO GO & THINGS TO DO FOR NEXT TIME: _____
_____
_____
_____

NOTES:

Date: _____	From: _____	Beginning Mileage: _____
Weather: ☀ ⛅ ☂ ❄ 🌡 🌡 📢 ☁	To: _____ Route Taken: _____ _____	Ending Mileage: _____ Total Miles Traveled: _____

Campground Information

Name: _____
Address: _____
Phone: _____

Site # _____ $ _____ ☐ Day ☐ Week ☐ Month
- ☐ First Visit ☐ Return Visit ☐ Easy Access
- ☐ Site Level ☐ Back-in ☐ Pull-through
- ☐ 15 amp ☐ 30 amp ☐ 50 amp
- ☐ Water ☐ Sewer ☐ Shade ☐ Sun
- ☐ Paved ☐ Sand / Grass ☐ Gravel
- ☐ Picnic Table ☐ Fire ring ☐ Trees ☐ Lawn
- ☐ Patio ☐ Kid Friendly ☐ Pet Friendly
- ☐ Store ☐ Cafe ☐ Firewood
- ☐ Ice ☐ Secuiryt ☐ Quiet ☐ Noisy

Our Rating: ☆ ☆ ☆ ☆ ☆
GPS: _____
Altitude: _____
Cell Service / Carrier: _____
- ☐ Antenna Reception ☐ Satellite TV ☐ Cable TV
- ☐ Wifi Available ☐ Free ☐ Fee $_____

Memberships: _____
Amenities: _____

Location	☺ 😐 ☹	Water Pressure	☺ 😐 ☹
Restrooms	☺ 😐 ☹	Laundry	☺ 😐 ☹
Pool	☺ 😐 ☹	Hot Tub	☺ 😐 ☹

Places Visited / Activities: _____
_____
_____
_____

People Met / New Friends: _____
_____
_____
_____

Food, Dining & Restaurants: _____
_____
_____
_____

Highlights / Memorable Events: _____
_____
_____
_____

Places To Go & Things To Do for Next Time: _____
_____
_____
_____

NOTES:

Date: _____

Weather:

From: _____

To: _____

Route Taken: _____
_____

Beginning Mileage: _____

Ending Mileage: _____

Total Miles Traveled: _____

Campground Information

Name: _____
Address: _____
Phone: _____

Site # _____ $ _____ ☐ Day ☐ Week ☐ Month

☐ First Visit   ☐ Return Visit   ☐ Easy Access
☐ Site Level   ☐ Back-in   ☐ Pull-through
☐ 15 amp   ☐ 30 amp   ☐ 50 amp
☐ Water   ☐ Sewer   ☐ Shade   ☐ Sun
☐ Paved   ☐ Sand / Grass   ☐ Gravel
☐ Picnic Table   ☐ Fire ring   ☐ Trees   ☐ Lawn
☐ Patio   ☐ Kid Friendly   ☐ Pet Friendly
☐ Store   ☐ Cafe   ☐ Firewood
☐ Ice   ☐ Secuiryt   ☐ Quiet   ☐ Noisy

Our Rating: ☆ ☆ ☆ ☆ ☆
GPS: _____
Altitude: _____
Cell Service / Carrier: _____
☐ Antenna Reception   ☐ Satellite TV   ☐ Cable TV
☐ Wifi Available   ☐ Free ☐ Fee $ _____
Memberships: _____
Amenities: _____

Location	☺	😐	☹	Water Pressure	☺	😐	☹
Restrooms	☺	😐	☹	Laundry	☺	😐	☹
Pool	☺	😐	☹	Hot Tub	☺	😐	☹

Places Visited / Activities: _____
_____
_____
_____

People Met / New Friends: _____
_____
_____
_____

Food, Dining & Restaurants: _____
_____
_____
_____

Highlights / Memorable Events: _____
_____
_____
_____

Places To Go & Things To Do for Next Time: _____
_____
_____
_____

Notes:

Date: _____　　From: _____　　Beginning Mileage: _____

Weather: ☀ ⛅ ☔ ❄　　To: _____　　Ending Mileage: _____

🌡 🌡 🚩 💭　　Route Taken: _____　　Total Miles Traveled: _____

CAMPGROUND INFORMATION

Our Rating: ☆ ☆ ☆ ☆ ☆

Name: _____

Address: _____　　GPS: _____

Phone: _____　　Altitude: _____

Site # _____ $ _____ ☐ Day ☐ Week ☐ Month　　Cell Service / Carrier: _____

☐ First Visit	☐ Return Visit	☐ Easy Access	☐ Antenna Reception	☐ Satellite TV	☐ Cable TV
☐ Site Level	☐ Back-in	☐ Pull-through	☐ Wifi Available	☐ Free ☐ Fee	$_____
☐ 15 amp	☐ 30 amp	☐ 50 amp			
☐ Water	☐ Sewer	☐ Shade ☐ Sun	Memberships: _____		
☐ Paved	☐ Sand / Grass	☐ Gravel	Ammenities: _____		
☐ Picnic Table	☐ Fire ring	☐ Trees ☐ Lawn	Location ☺ 😐 ☹　Water Pressure ☺ 😐 ☹		
☐ Patio	☐ Kid Friendly	☐ Pet Friendly	Restrooms ☺ 😐 ☹　Laundry ☺ 😐 ☹		
☐ Store	☐ Cafe	☐ Firewood	Pool ☺ 😐 ☹　Hot Tub ☺ 😐 ☹		
☐ Ice	☐ Secuiryt	☐ Quiet ☐ Noisy			

PLACES VISITED / ACTIVITIES: _____

_____

_____

_____

PEOPLE MET / NEW FRIENDS: _____

_____

_____

_____

FOOD, DINING & RESTAURANTS: _____

_____

_____

_____

HIGHLIGHTS / MEMORABLE EVENTS: _____

_____

_____

_____

PLACES TO GO & THINGS TO DO FOR NEXT TIME: _____

_____

_____

_____

NOTES:

Date: _____   From: _____   Beginning Mileage: _____

Weather: To: _____   Ending Mileage: _____

                         Route Taken: _____   Total Miles Traveled: _____
                         _____

Campground Information

Name: _____   Our Rating: ☆ ☆ ☆ ☆ ☆
Address: _____   GPS: _____
Phone: _____   Altitude: _____

Site # _____ $ _____   ☐ Day ☐ Week ☐ Month   Cell Service / Carrier: _____
☐ First Visit   ☐ Return Visit   ☐ Easy Access   ☐ Antenna Reception   ☐ Satellite TV   ☐ Cable TV
☐ Site Level   ☐ Back-in   ☐ Pull-through   ☐ Wifi Available   ☐ Free ☐ Fee $_____
☐ 15 amp   ☐ 30 amp   ☐ 50 amp   Memberships: _____
☐ Water   ☐ Sewer   ☐ Shade ☐ Sun   Ammenities: _____
☐ Paved   ☐ Sand / Grass   ☐ Gravel
☐ Picnic Table   ☐ Fire ring   ☐ Trees ☐ Lawn   Location   ☺ 😐 ☹   Water Pressure ☺ 😐 ☹
☐ Patio   ☐ Kid Friendly   ☐ Pet Friendly   Restrooms   ☺ 😐 ☹   Laundry   ☺ 😐 ☹
☐ Store   ☐ Cafe   ☐ Firewood   Pool   ☺ 😐 ☹   Hot Tub   ☺ 😐 ☹
☐ Ice   ☐ Secuiryt   ☐ Quiet ☐ Noisy

Places Visited / Activities: _____

_____
_____
_____

People Met / New Friends: _____

_____
_____
_____

Food, Dining & Restaurants: _____

_____
_____
_____

Highlights / Memorable Events: _____

_____
_____
_____

Places To Go & Things To Do for Next Time: _____

_____
_____
_____

NOTES:

Date: _____	From: _____	Beginning Mileage: _____
Weather: ☀ ⛅ ☔ ❄ 🌡 ❄ 🌬 🌫	To: _____ Route Taken: _____ _____	Ending Mileage: _____ Total Miles Traveled: _____

Campground Information

Name: _____
Address: _____
Phone: _____

Our Rating: ☆ ☆ ☆ ☆ ☆
GPS: _____
Altitude: _____

Site # _____ $ _____ ☐ Day ☐ Week ☐ Month

Cell Service / Carrier: _____

☐ First Visit	☐ Return Visit	☐ Easy Access	☐ Antenna Reception	☐ Satellite TV	☐ Cable TV
☐ Site Level	☐ Back-in	☐ Pull-through	☐ Wifi Available	☐ Free ☐ Fee	$_____
☐ 15 amp	☐ 30 amp	☐ 50 amp			
☐ Water	☐ Sewer	☐ Shade ☐ Sun	Memberships: _____		
☐ Paved	☐ Sand / Grass	☐ Gravel	Amenities: _____		
☐ Picnic Table	☐ Fire ring	☐ Trees ☐ Lawn	Location ☺ 😐 ☹	Water Pressure	☺ 😐 ☹
☐ Patio	☐ Kid Friendly	☐ Pet Friendly	Restrooms ☺ 😐 ☹	Laundry	☺ 😐 ☹
☐ Store	☐ Cafe	☐ Firewood	Pool ☺ 😐 ☹	Hot Tub	☺ 😐 ☹
☐ Ice	☐ Secuiryt	☐ Quiet ☐ Noisy			

Places Visited / Activities: _____

_____
_____
_____

People Met / New Friends: _____

_____
_____
_____

Food, Dining & Restaurants: _____

_____
_____
_____

Highlights / Memorable Events: _____

_____
_____
_____

Places To Go & Things To Do for Next Time: _____

_____
_____
_____

NOTES:

Date: _____

Weather:

From: _____
To: _____
Route Taken: _____
_____

Beginning Mileage: _____
Ending Mileage: _____
Total Miles Traveled: _____

Campground Information

Name: _____
Address: _____
Phone: _____

Our Rating: ☆ ☆ ☆ ☆ ☆
GPS: _____
Altitude: _____

Site # _____ $ _____ ☐ Day ☐ Week ☐ Month

Cell Service / Carrier: _____

☐ First Visit   ☐ Return Visit   ☐ Easy Access
☐ Site Level   ☐ Back-in   ☐ Pull-through
☐ 15 amp   ☐ 30 amp   ☐ 50 amp
☐ Water   ☐ Sewer   ☐ Shade   ☐ Sun
☐ Paved   ☐ Sand / Grass   ☐ Gravel
☐ Picnic Table   ☐ Fire ring   ☐ Trees   ☐ Lawn
☐ Patio   ☐ Kid Friendly   ☐ Pet Friendly
☐ Store   ☐ Cafe   ☐ Firewood
☐ Ice   ☐ Security   ☐ Quiet   ☐ Noisy

☐ Antenna Reception   ☐ Satellite TV   ☐ Cable TV
☐ Wifi Available   ☐ Free ☐ Fee $_____

Memberships: _____
Ammenities: _____

	☺	😐	☹		☺	😐	☹
Location	☺	😐	☹	Water Pressure	☺	😐	☹
Restrooms	☺	😐	☹	Laundry	☺	😐	☹
Pool	☺	😐	☹	Hot Tub	☺	😐	☹

Places Visited / Activities: _____
_____
_____
_____

People Met / New Friends: _____
_____
_____
_____

Food, Dining & Restaurants: _____
_____
_____
_____

Highlights / Memorable Events: _____
_____
_____
_____

Places To Go & Things To Do for Next Time: _____
_____
_____
_____

NOTES:

Date: _____	From: _____	Beginning Mileage: _____
Weather:	To: _____	Ending Mileage: _____
	Route Taken: _____	Total Miles Traveled: _____

Campground Information

Name: _____

Address: _____

Phone: _____

Site # _____ $ _____ ☐ Day ☐ Week ☐ Month

☐ First Visit   ☐ Return Visit   ☐ Easy Access
☐ Site Level   ☐ Back-in   ☐ Pull-through
☐ 15 amp   ☐ 30 amp   ☐ 50 amp
☐ Water   ☐ Sewer   ☐ Shade   ☐ Sun
☐ Paved   ☐ Sand / Grass   ☐ Gravel
☐ Picnic Table ☐ Fire ring   ☐ Trees   ☐ Lawn
☐ Patio   ☐ Kid Friendly   ☐ Pet Friendly
☐ Store   ☐ Cafe   ☐ Firewood
☐ Ice   ☐ Secuiryt   ☐ Quiet   ☐ Noisy

Our Rating: ☆ ☆ ☆ ☆ ☆

GPS: _____

Altitude: _____

Cell Service / Carrier: _____

☐ Antenna Reception ☐ Satellite TV ☐ Cable TV
☐ Wifi Available   ☐ Free ☐ Fee $_____

Memberships: _____

Ammenities: _____

Location	☺ ☹ ☹	Water Pressure	☺ ☹ ☹
Restrooms	☺ ☹ ☹	Laundry	☺ ☹ ☹
Pool	☺ ☹ ☹	Hot Tub	☺ ☹ ☹

Places Visited / Activities: _____

People Met / New Friends: _____

Food, Dining & Restaurants: _____

Highlights / Memorable Events: _____

Places To Go & Things To Do for Next Time: _____

NOTES:

Date: _____ From: _____ Beginning Mileage: _____

Weather: To: _____ Ending Mileage: _____

Route Taken: _____

_____ Total Miles Traveled: _____

Campground Information

Name: _____

Address: _____

Phone: _____

Site #_____ $_____ ☐ Day ☐ Week ☐ Month

☐ First Visit   ☐ Return Visit   ☐ Easy Access
☐ Site Level   ☐ Back-in   ☐ Pull-through
☐ 15 amp   ☐ 30 amp   ☐ 50 amp
☐ Water   ☐ Sewer   ☐ Shade   ☐ Sun
☐ Paved   ☐ Sand / Grass   ☐ Gravel
☐ Picnic Table   ☐ Fire ring   ☐ Trees   ☐ Lawn
☐ Patio   ☐ Kid Friendly   ☐ Pet Friendly
☐ Store   ☐ Cafe   ☐ Firewood
☐ Ice   ☐ Secuiryt   ☐ Quiet   ☐ Noisy

Our Rating: ☆ ☆ ☆ ☆ ☆

GPS: _____

Altitude: _____

Cell Service / Carrier: _____

☐ Antenna Reception   ☐ Satellite TV   ☐ Cable TV
☐ Wifi Available   ☐ Free ☐ Fee $_____

Memberships: _____

Ammenities: _____

Location   ☺ ☺ ☹   Water Pressure ☺ ☺ ☹
Restrooms ☺ ☺ ☹   Laundry   ☺ ☺ ☹
Pool   ☺ ☺ ☹   Hot Tub   ☺ ☺ ☹

Places Visited / Activities: _____

_____

_____

_____

People Met / New Friends: _____

_____

_____

_____

Food, Dining & Restaurants: _____

_____

_____

_____

Highlights / Memorable Events: _____

_____

_____

_____

Places To Go & Things To Do for Next Time: _____

_____

_____

_____

NOTES:

Date: _____ From: _____ Beginning Mileage: _____

Weather: To: _____ Ending Mileage: _____

Route Taken: _____ Total Miles Traveled: _____
_____

Campground Information

Name: _____

Address: _____

Phone: _____

Site # _____ $ _____ ☐ Day ☐ Week ☐ Month

☐ First Visit   ☐ Return Visit   ☐ Easy Access
☐ Site Level   ☐ Back-in   ☐ Pull-through
☐ 15 amp   ☐ 30 amp   ☐ 50 amp
☐ Water   ☐ Sewer   ☐ Shade   ☐ Sun
☐ Paved   ☐ Sand / Grass   ☐ Gravel
☐ Picnic Table   ☐ Fire ring   ☐ Trees   ☐ Lawn
☐ Patio   ☐ Kid Friendly   ☐ Pet Friendly
☐ Store   ☐ Cafe   ☐ Firewood
☐ Ice   ☐ Secuiryt   ☐ Quiet   ☐ Noisy

Our Rating: ☆ ☆ ☆ ☆ ☆

GPS: _____

Altitude: _____

Cell Service / Carrier: _____

☐ Antenna Reception   ☐ Satellite TV   ☐ Cable TV
☐ Wifi Available   ☐ Free ☐ Fee $_____

Memberships: _____

Ammenities: _____

Location   ☺ 😐 ☹   Water Pressure ☺ 😐 ☹
Restrooms   ☺ 😐 ☹   Laundry   ☺ 😐 ☹
Pool   ☺ 😐 ☹   Hot Tub   ☺ 😐 ☹

Places Visited / Activities: _____
_____
_____
_____

People Met / New Friends: _____
_____
_____
_____

Food, Dining & Restaurants: _____
_____
_____
_____

Highlights / Memorable Events: _____
_____
_____

Places To Go & Things To Do for Next Time: _____
_____
_____
_____

NOTES:

Date:	From:	Beginning Mileage:
Weather:	To:	Ending Mileage:
	Route Taken:	Total Miles Traveled:

Campground Information

Name: _____

Address: _____

Phone: _____

Site # _____ $ _____ ☐ Day ☐ Week ☐ Month

☐ First Visit ☐ Return Visit ☐ Easy Access
☐ Site Level ☐ Back-in ☐ Pull-through
☐ 15 amp ☐ 30 amp ☐ 50 amp
☐ Water ☐ Sewer ☐ Shade ☐ Sun
☐ Paved ☐ Sand / Grass ☐ Gravel
☐ Picnic Table ☐ Fire ring ☐ Trees ☐ Lawn
☐ Patio ☐ Kid Friendly ☐ Pet Friendly
☐ Store ☐ Cafe ☐ Firewood
☐ Ice ☐ Secuiryt ☐ Quiet ☐ Noisy

Our Rating: ☆ ☆ ☆ ☆ ☆

GPS: _____

Altitude: _____

Cell Service / Carrier: _____

☐ Antenna Reception ☐ Satellite TV ☐ Cable TV
☐ Wifi Available ☐ Free ☐ Fee $ _____

Memberships: _____

Ammenities: _____

Location	☺	😐	☹	Water Pressure	☺	😐	☹
Restrooms	☺	😐	☹	Laundry	☺	😐	☹
Pool	☺	😐	☹	Hot Tub	☺	😐	☹

Places Visited / Activities: _____

_____

_____

People Met / New Friends: _____

_____

_____

Food, Dining & Restaurants: _____

_____

_____

Highlights / Memorable Events: _____

_____

_____

Places To Go & Things To Do for Next Time: _____

_____

_____

NOTES:

Date: _____

Weather:

From: _____
To: _____
Route Taken: _____
_____

Beginning Mileage: _____

Ending Mileage: _____

Total Miles Traveled: _____

Campground Information

Name: _____
Address: _____
Phone: _____

Site # _____ $ _____ ☐ Day ☐ Week ☐ Month
☐ First Visit   ☐ Return Visit   ☐ Easy Access
☐ Site Level   ☐ Back-in   ☐ Pull-through
☐ 15 amp   ☐ 30 amp   ☐ 50 amp
☐ Water   ☐ Sewer   ☐ Shade   ☐ Sun
☐ Paved   ☐ Sand / Grass   ☐ Gravel
☐ Picnic Table   ☐ Fire ring   ☐ Trees   ☐ Lawn
☐ Patio   ☐ Kid Friendly   ☐ Pet Friendly
☐ Store   ☐ Cafe   ☐ Firewood
☐ Ice   ☐ Secuiryt   ☐ Quiet   ☐ Noisy

Our Rating: ☆ ☆ ☆ ☆ ☆
GPS: _____
Altitude: _____
Cell Service / Carrier: _____
☐ Antenna Reception   ☐ Satellite TV   ☐ Cable TV
☐ Wifi Available   ☐ Free ☐ Fee $_____
Memberships: _____
Ammenities: _____

Location	☺	😐	☹	Water Pressure	☺	😐	☹
Restrooms	☺	😐	☹	Laundry	☺	😐	☹
Pool	☺	😐	☹	Hot Tub	☺	😐	☹

Places Visited / Activities: _____
_____
_____
_____

People Met / New Friends: _____
_____
_____
_____

Food, Dining & Restaurants: _____
_____
_____
_____

Highlights / Memorable Events: _____
_____
_____
_____

Places To Go & Things To Do for Next Time: _____
_____
_____
_____

NOTES:

Date: _____
Weather:

From: _____
To: _____
Route Taken: _____
_____

Beginning Mileage: _____
Ending Mileage: _____
Total Miles Traveled: _____

Campground Information

Name: _____
Address: _____
Phone: _____

Our Rating: ☆ ☆ ☆ ☆
GPS: _____
Altitude: _____

Site # _____ $ _____ ☐ Day ☐ Week ☐ Month
☐ First Visit   ☐ Return Visit   ☐ Easy Access
☐ Site Level   ☐ Back-in   ☐ Pull-through
☐ 15 amp   ☐ 30 amp   ☐ 50 amp
☐ Water   ☐ Sewer   ☐ Shade   ☐ Sun
☐ Paved   ☐ Sand / Grass   ☐ Gravel
☐ Picnic Table   ☐ Fire ring   ☐ Trees   ☐ Lawn
☐ Patio   ☐ Kid Friendly   ☐ Pet Friendly
☐ Store   ☐ Cafe   ☐ Firewood
☐ Ice   ☐ Secuiryt   ☐ Quiet   ☐ Noisy

Cell Service / Carrier: _____
☐ Antenna Reception   ☐ Satellite TV   ☐ Cable TV
☐ Wifi Available   ☐ Free ☐ Fee $_____
Memberships: _____
Amenities: _____

Location   ☺ ☺ ☹   Water Pressure   ☺ ☺ ☹
Restrooms   ☺ ☺ ☹   Laundry   ☺ ☺ ☹
Pool   ☺ ☺ ☹   Hot Tub   ☺ ☺ ☹

Places Visited / Activities: _____
_____
_____
_____

People Met / New Friends: _____
_____
_____
_____

Food, Dining & Restaurants: _____
_____
_____
_____

Highlights / Memorable Events: _____
_____
_____
_____

Places To Go & Things To Do for Next Time: _____
_____
_____
_____

NOTES:

Date:	From:	Beginning Mileage:
Weather:	To:	Ending Mileage:
	Route Taken:	Total Miles Traveled:

Campground Information

Name: _____

Address: _____

Phone: _____

Site # _____ $ _____ ☐ Day ☐ Week ☐ Month

☐ First Visit   ☐ Return Visit   ☐ Easy Access
☐ Site Level   ☐ Back-in   ☐ Pull-through
☐ 15 amp   ☐ 30 amp   ☐ 50 amp
☐ Water   ☐ Sewer   ☐ Shade   ☐ Sun
☐ Paved   ☐ Sand / Grass   ☐ Gravel
☐ Picnic Table ☐ Fire ring   ☐ Trees   ☐ Lawn
☐ Patio   ☐ Kid Friendly   ☐ Pet Friendly
☐ Store   ☐ Cafe   ☐ Firewood
☐ Ice   ☐ Secuiryt   ☐ Quiet   ☐ Noisy

Our Rating: ☆ ☆ ☆ ☆ ☆

GPS: _____

Altitude: _____

Cell Service / Carrier: _____

☐ Antenna Reception ☐ Satellite TV ☐ Cable TV
☐ Wifi Available   ☐ Free ☐ Fee $_____

Memberships: _____

Amenities: _____

Location	☺	😐	☹	Water Pressure	☺	😐	☹
Restrooms	☺	😐	☹	Laundry	☺	😐	☹
Pool	☺	😐	☹	Hot Tub	☺	😐	☹

Places Visited / Activities: _____

_____

_____

_____

People Met / New Friends: _____

_____

_____

_____

Food, Dining & Restaurants: _____

_____

_____

_____

Highlights / Memorable Events: _____

_____

_____

_____

Places To Go & Things To Do for Next Time: _____

_____

_____

_____

Notes:

Date: _____

Weather:

From: _____
To: _____
Route Taken: _____
_____

Beginning Mileage: _____

Ending Mileage: _____

Total Miles Traveled: _____

Campground Information

Name: _____
Address: _____
Phone: _____

Site # _____ $ _____ ☐ Day ☐ Week ☐ Month

- ☐ First Visit
- ☐ Site Level
- ☐ 15 amp
- ☐ Water
- ☐ Paved
- ☐ Picnic Table
- ☐ Patio
- ☐ Store
- ☐ Ice

- ☐ Return Visit
- ☐ Back-in
- ☐ 30 amp
- ☐ Sewer
- ☐ Sand / Grass
- ☐ Fire ring
- ☐ Kid Friendly
- ☐ Cafe
- ☐ Secuiryt

- ☐ Easy Access
- ☐ Pull-through
- ☐ 50 amp
- ☐ Shade ☐ Sun
- ☐ Gravel
- ☐ Trees ☐ Lawn
- ☐ Pet Friendly
- ☐ Firewood
- ☐ Quiet ☐ Noisy

Our Rating: ☆ ☆ ☆ ☆ ☆

GPS: _____
Altitude: _____
Cell Service / Carrier: _____

- ☐ Antenna Reception ☐ Satellite TV ☐ Cable TV
- ☐ Wifi Available ☐ Free ☐ Fee $_____

Memberships: _____
Ammenities: _____

Location	☺	😐	☹	Water Pressure	☺	😐	☹
Restrooms	☺	😐	☹	Laundry	☺	😐	☹
Pool	☺	😐	☹	Hot Tub	☺	😐	☹

Places Visited / Activities: _____
_____
_____
_____

People Met / New Friends: _____
_____
_____
_____

Food, Dining & Restaurants: _____
_____
_____
_____

Highlights / Memorable Events: _____
_____
_____
_____

Places To Go & Things To Do for Next Time: _____
_____
_____
_____

Notes:

Date: _____

Weather:

From: _____

To: _____

Route Taken: _____
_____

Beginning Mileage: _____

Ending Mileage: _____

Total Miles Traveled: _____

Campground Information

Name: _____

Address: _____

Phone: _____

Site # _____ $ _____ ☐ Day ☐ Week ☐ Month

☐ First Visit ☐ Return Visit ☐ Easy Access
☐ Site Level ☐ Back-in ☐ Pull-through
☐ 15 amp ☐ 30 amp ☐ 50 amp
☐ Water ☐ Sewer ☐ Shade ☐ Sun
☐ Paved ☐ Sand / Grass ☐ Gravel
☐ Picnic Table ☐ Fire ring ☐ Trees ☐ Lawn
☐ Patio ☐ Kid Friendly ☐ Pet Friendly
☐ Store ☐ Cafe ☐ Firewood
☐ Ice ☐ Secuiryt ☐ Quiet ☐ Noisy

Our Rating: ☆ ☆ ☆ ☆ ☆

GPS: _____

Altitude: _____

Cell Service / Carrier: _____

☐ Antenna Reception ☐ Satellite TV ☐ Cable TV
☐ Wifi Available ☐ Free ☐ Fee $_____

Memberships: _____

Ammenities: _____

Location	☺	😐	☹	Water Pressure	☺	😐	☹
Restrooms	☺	😐	☹	Laundry	☺	😐	☹
Pool	☺	😐	☹	Hot Tub	☺	😐	☹

Places Visited / Activities:
_____
_____
_____
_____

People Met / New Friends:
_____
_____
_____
_____

Food, Dining & Restaurants:
_____
_____
_____
_____

Highlights / Memorable Events:
_____
_____
_____
_____

Places To Go & Things To Do for Next Time:
_____
_____
_____
_____

Notes:

Date: _____ From: _____ Beginning Mileage: _____

Weather: To: _____ Ending Mileage: _____

Route Taken: _____ Total Miles Traveled: _____
_____

CAMPGROUND INFORMATION

	Our Rating: ☆ ☆ ☆ ☆
Name: _____	
Address: _____	GPS: _____
Phone: _____	Altitude: _____

Site # _____ $ _____ ☐ Day ☐ Week ☐ Month   Cell Service / Carrier: _____

☐ First Visit   ☐ Return Visit   ☐ Easy Access   ☐ Antenna Reception   ☐ Satellite TV   ☐ Cable TV
☐ Site Level   ☐ Back-in   ☐ Pull-through   ☐ Wifi Available   ☐ Free ☐ Fee $_____
☐ 15 amp   ☐ 30 amp   ☐ 50 amp
☐ Water   ☐ Sewer   ☐ Shade ☐ Sun   Memberships: _____
☐ Paved   ☐ Sand / Grass   ☐ Gravel   Ammenities: _____
☐ Picnic Table   ☐ Fire ring   ☐ Trees ☐ Lawn   Location   ☺ ☹ ☹   Water Pressure ☺ ☹ ☹
☐ Patio   ☐ Kid Friendly   ☐ Pet Friendly   Restrooms   ☺ ☹ ☹   Laundry   ☺ ☹ ☹
☐ Store   ☐ Cafe   ☐ Firewood   Pool   ☺ ☹ ☹   Hot Tub   ☺ ☹ ☹
☐ Ice   ☐ Secuiryt   ☐ Quiet ☐ Noisy

PLACES VISITED / ACTIVITIES: _____
_____
_____
_____

PEOPLE MET / NEW FRIENDS: _____
_____
_____
_____

FOOD, DINING & RESTAURANTS: _____
_____
_____
_____

HIGHLIGHTS / MEMORABLE EVENTS: _____
_____
_____
_____

PLACES TO GO & THINGS TO DO FOR NEXT TIME: _____
_____
_____
_____

Notes:

Date: _____

From: _____

Weather:

To: _____

Route Taken: _____

_____

Beginning Mileage: _____

Ending Mileage: _____

Total Miles Traveled: _____

Campground Information

Name: _____

Address: _____

Phone: _____

Site # _____ $ _____ ☐ Day ☐ Week ☐ Month

☐ First Visit   ☐ Return Visit   ☐ Easy Access
☐ Site Level   ☐ Back-in   ☐ Pull-through
☐ 15 amp   ☐ 30 amp   ☐ 50 amp
☐ Water   ☐ Sewer   ☐ Shade ☐ Sun
☐ Paved   ☐ Sand / Grass   ☐ Gravel
☐ Picnic Table   ☐ Fire ring   ☐ Trees ☐ Lawn
☐ Patio   ☐ Kid Friendly   ☐ Pet Friendly
☐ Store   ☐ Cafe   ☐ Firewood
☐ Ice   ☐ Secuiryt   ☐ Quiet ☐ Noisy

Our Rating: ☆ ☆ ☆ ☆ ☆

GPS: _____

Altitude: _____

Cell Service / Carrier: _____

☐ Antenna Reception   ☐ Satellite TV   ☐ Cable TV
☐ Wifi Available   ☐ Free ☐ Fee $_____

Memberships: _____

Ammenities: _____

Location	☺	😐	☹	Water Pressure	☺	😐	☹
Restrooms	☺	😐	☹	Laundry	☺	😐	☹
Pool	☺	😐	☹	Hot Tub	☺	😐	☹

Places Visited / Activities: _____

_____

_____

_____

People Met / New Friends: _____

_____

_____

_____

Food, Dining & Restaurants: _____

_____

_____

_____

Highlights / Memorable Events: _____

_____

_____

_____

Places To Go & Things To Do for Next Time: _____

_____

_____

_____

NOTES:

Date: _____
From: _____
Weather:
To: _____
Route Taken: _____
_____

Beginning Mileage: _____
Ending Mileage: _____
Total Miles Traveled: _____

Campground Information

Name: _____
Address: _____
Phone: _____
Site # _____ $ _____ ☐ Day ☐ Week ☐ Month

- ☐ First Visit
- ☐ Site Level
- ☐ 15 amp
- ☐ Water
- ☐ Paved
- ☐ Picnic Table
- ☐ Patio
- ☐ Store
- ☐ Ice

- ☐ Return Visit
- ☐ Back-in
- ☐ 30 amp
- ☐ Sewer
- ☐ Sand / Grass
- ☐ Fire ring
- ☐ Kid Friendly
- ☐ Cafe
- ☐ Secuiryt

- ☐ Easy Access
- ☐ Pull-through
- ☐ 50 amp
- ☐ Shade ☐ Sun
- ☐ Gravel
- ☐ Trees ☐ Lawn
- ☐ Pet Friendly
- ☐ Firewood
- ☐ Quiet ☐ Noisy

Our Rating: ☆ ☆ ☆ ☆ ☆
GPS: _____
Altitude: _____
Cell Service / Carrier: _____
- ☐ Antenna Reception ☐ Satellite TV ☐ Cable TV
- ☐ Wifi Available ☐ Free ☐ Fee $_____

Memberships: _____
Ammenities: _____

Location	☺	😐	☹	Water Pressure	☺	😐	☹
Restrooms	☺	😐	☹	Laundry	☺	😐	☹
Pool	☺	😐	☹	Hot Tub	☺	😐	☹

Places Visited / Activities:
_____
_____
_____

People Met / New Friends:
_____
_____
_____

Food, Dining & Restaurants:
_____
_____
_____

Highlights / Memorable Events:
_____
_____
_____

Places To Go & Things To Do for Next Time:
_____
_____
_____

NOTES:

Date:	From:	Beginning Mileage:
Weather:	To:	Ending Mileage:
	Route Taken:	Total Miles Traveled:

Campground Information

Name: _____

Address: _____

Phone: _____

Our Rating: ☆ ☆ ☆ ☆ ☆

GPS: _____

Altitude: _____

Site # _____ $ _____ ☐ Day ☐ Week ☐ Month

Cell Service / Carrier: _____

- ☐ First Visit
- ☐ Site Level
- ☐ 15 amp
- ☐ Water
- ☐ Paved
- ☐ Picnic Table
- ☐ Patio
- ☐ Store
- ☐ Ice

- ☐ Return Visit
- ☐ Back-in
- ☐ 30 amp
- ☐ Sewer
- ☐ Sand / Grass
- ☐ Fire ring
- ☐ Kid Friendly
- ☐ Cafe
- ☐ Secuiryt

- ☐ Easy Access
- ☐ Pull-through
- ☐ 50 amp
- ☐ Shade ☐ Sun
- ☐ Gravel
- ☐ Trees ☐ Lawn
- ☐ Pet Friendly
- ☐ Firewood
- ☐ Quiet ☐ Noisy

- ☐ Antenna Reception ☐ Satellite TV ☐ Cable TV
- ☐ Wifi Available ☐ Free ☐ Fee $_____

Memberships: _____

Ammenities: _____

Location	☺	😐	☹	Water Pressure	☺	😐	☹
Restrooms	☺	😐	☹	Laundry	☺	😐	☹
Pool	☺	😐	☹	Hot Tub	☺	😐	☹

Places Visited / Activities: _____

People Met / New Friends: _____

Food, Dining & Restaurants: _____

Highlights / Memorable Events: _____

Places To Go & Things To Do for Next Time: _____

NOTES:

| Date: _____ | From: _____ | Beginning Mileage: _____ |
| Weather: ☀ ⛅ ☂ ❄ 🌡 ❄ 🚩 ☁ | To: _____
Route Taken: _____
_____ | Ending Mileage: _____

Total Miles Traveled: _____ |

Campground Information

Name: _____
Address: _____
Phone: _____

Our Rating: ☆ ☆ ☆ ☆ ☆
GPS: _____
Altitude: _____

Site # _____ $ _____ ☐ Day ☐ Week ☐ Month

☐ First Visit ☐ Return Visit ☐ Easy Access
☐ Site Level ☐ Back-in ☐ Pull-through
☐ 15 amp ☐ 30 amp ☐ 50 amp
☐ Water ☐ Sewer ☐ Shade ☐ Sun
☐ Paved ☐ Sand / Grass ☐ Gravel
☐ Picnic Table ☐ Fire ring ☐ Trees ☐ Lawn
☐ Patio ☐ Kid Friendly ☐ Pet Friendly
☐ Store ☐ Cafe ☐ Firewood
☐ Ice ☐ Secuiryt ☐ Quiet ☐ Noisy

Cell Service / Carrier: _____
☐ Antenna Reception ☐ Satellite TV ☐ Cable TV
☐ Wifi Available ☐ Free ☐ Fee $ _____
Memberships: _____
Ammenities: _____

Location	🙂 😐 🙁	Water Pressure	🙂 😐 🙁
Restrooms	🙂 😐 🙁	Laundry	🙂 😐 🙁
Pool	🙂 😐 🙁	Hot Tub	🙂 😐 🙁

Places Visited / Activities: _____
_____
_____
_____

People Met / New Friends: _____
_____
_____
_____

Food, Dining & Restaurants: _____
_____
_____
_____

Highlights / Memorable Events: _____
_____
_____
_____

Places To Go & Things To Do for Next Time: _____
_____
_____
_____

Notes:

Date: _____
Weather:
From: _____
To: _____
Route Taken: _____
_____

Beginning Mileage: _____
Ending Mileage: _____
Total Miles Traveled: _____

Campground Information

Name: _____
Address: _____
Phone: _____

Our Rating: ☆ ☆ ☆ ☆ ☆
GPS: _____
Altitude: _____

Site # _____ $ _____ ☐ Day ☐ Week ☐ Month
☐ First Visit   ☐ Return Visit   ☐ Easy Access
☐ Site Level   ☐ Back-in   ☐ Pull-through
☐ 15 amp   ☐ 30 amp   ☐ 50 amp
☐ Water   ☐ Sewer   ☐ Shade   ☐ Sun
☐ Paved   ☐ Sand / Grass   ☐ Gravel
☐ Picnic Table   ☐ Fire ring   ☐ Trees   ☐ Lawn
☐ Patio   ☐ Kid Friendly   ☐ Pet Friendly
☐ Store   ☐ Cafe   ☐ Firewood
☐ Ice   ☐ Secuiryt   ☐ Quiet   ☐ Noisy

Cell Service / Carrier: _____
☐ Antenna Reception   ☐ Satellite TV   ☐ Cable TV
☐ Wifi Available   ☐ Free ☐ Fee $ _____
Memberships: _____
Ammenities: _____

Location	☺	😐	☹	Water Pressure	☺	😐	☹
Restrooms	☺	😐	☹	Laundry	☺	😐	☹
Pool	☺	😐	☹	Hot Tub	☺	😐	☹

Places Visited / Activities: _____
_____
_____
_____

People Met / New Friends: _____
_____
_____
_____

Food, Dining & Restaurants: _____
_____
_____
_____

Highlights / Memorable Events: _____
_____
_____
_____

Places To Go & Things To Do for Next Time: ___
_____
_____
_____

Notes:

Date: _____

Weather:

From: _____

To: _____

Route Taken: _____
_____

Beginning Mileage:
_____

Ending Mileage:
_____

Total Miles Traveled:
_____

Campground Information

Name: _____
Address: _____
Phone: _____

Site # _____ $ _____ ☐ Day ☐ Week ☐ Month

☐ First Visit   ☐ Return Visit   ☐ Easy Access
☐ Site Level   ☐ Back-in   ☐ Pull-through
☐ 15 amp   ☐ 30 amp   ☐ 50 amp
☐ Water   ☐ Sewer   ☐ Shade   ☐ Sun
☐ Paved   ☐ Sand / Grass   ☐ Gravel
☐ Picnic Table   ☐ Fire ring   ☐ Trees   ☐ Lawn
☐ Patio   ☐ Kid Friendly   ☐ Pet Friendly
☐ Store   ☐ Cafe   ☐ Firewood
☐ Ice   ☐ Secuiryt   ☐ Quiet   ☐ Noisy

Our Rating: ☆ ☆ ☆ ☆ ☆
GPS: _____
Altitude: _____
Cell Service / Carrier: _____
☐ Antenna Reception   ☐ Satellite TV   ☐ Cable TV
☐ Wifi Available   ☐ Free ☐ Fee $_____
Memberships: _____
Ammenities: _____

Location	☺	😐	☹	Water Pressure	☺	😐	☹
Restrooms	☺	😐	☹	Laundry	☺	😐	☹
Pool	☺	😐	☹	Hot Tub	☺	😐	☹

Places Visited / Activities: _____
_____
_____
_____

People Met / New Friends: _____
_____
_____
_____

Food, Dining & Restaurants: _____
_____
_____
_____

Highlights / Memorable Events: _____
_____
_____
_____

Places To Go & Things To Do for Next Time: _____
_____
_____
_____

NOTES:

Date: _____

Weather:

From: _____
To: _____
Route Taken: _____
_____

Beginning Mileage: _____

Ending Mileage: _____

Total Miles Traveled: _____

Campground Information

Name: _____
Address: _____
Phone: _____

Site # _____ $ _____ ☐ Day ☐ Week ☐ Month
☐ First Visit   ☐ Return Visit   ☐ Easy Access
☐ Site Level   ☐ Back-in   ☐ Pull-through
☐ 15 amp   ☐ 30 amp   ☐ 50 amp
☐ Water   ☐ Sewer   ☐ Shade   ☐ Sun
☐ Paved   ☐ Sand / Grass   ☐ Gravel
☐ Picnic Table   ☐ Fire ring   ☐ Trees   ☐ Lawn
☐ Patio   ☐ Kid Friendly   ☐ Pet Friendly
☐ Store   ☐ Cafe   ☐ Firewood
☐ Ice   ☐ Secuiryt   ☐ Quiet   ☐ Noisy

Our Rating: ☆ ☆ ☆ ☆
GPS: _____
Altitude: _____
Cell Service / Carrier: _____
☐ Antenna Reception   ☐ Satellite TV   ☐ Cable TV
☐ Wifi Available   ☐ Free ☐ Fee $ _____
Memberships: _____
Ammenities: _____

Location	☺	😐	☹	Water Pressure	☺	😐	☹
Restrooms	☺	😐	☹	Laundry	☺	😐	☹
Pool	☺	😐	☹	Hot Tub	☺	😐	☹

Places Visited / Activities: _____
_____
_____
_____

People Met / New Friends: _____
_____
_____
_____

Food, Dining & Restaurants: _____
_____
_____
_____

Highlights / Memorable Events: _____
_____
_____
_____

Places To Go & Things To Do for Next Time: _____
_____
_____
_____

Notes:

Date: _____
Weather:

From: _____
To: _____
Route Taken: _____
_____

Beginning Mileage: _____
Ending Mileage: _____
Total Miles Traveled: _____

Campground Information

Name: _____
Address: _____
Phone: _____

Our Rating: ☆ ☆ ☆ ☆ ☆
GPS: _____
Altitude: _____

Site # _____ $ _____ ☐ Day ☐ Week ☐ Month
☐ First Visit   ☐ Return Visit   ☐ Easy Access
☐ Site Level   ☐ Back-in   ☐ Pull-through
☐ 15 amp   ☐ 30 amp   ☐ 50 amp
☐ Water   ☐ Sewer   ☐ Shade   ☐ Sun
☐ Paved   ☐ Sand / Grass   ☐ Gravel
☐ Picnic Table   ☐ Fire ring   ☐ Trees   ☐ Lawn
☐ Patio   ☐ Kid Friendly   ☐ Pet Friendly
☐ Store   ☐ Cafe   ☐ Firewood
☐ Ice   ☐ Secuiryt   ☐ Quiet   ☐ Noisy

Cell Service / Carrier: _____
☐ Antenna Reception   ☐ Satellite TV   ☐ Cable TV
☐ Wifi Available   ☐ Free ☐ Fee $_____
Memberships: _____
Ammenities: _____

Location	☺	😐	☹	Water Pressure	☺	😐	☹
Restrooms	☺	😐	☹	Laundry	☺	😐	☹
Pool	☺	😐	☹	Hot Tub	☺	😐	☹

Places Visited / Activities: _____
_____
_____
_____

People Met / New Friends: _____
_____
_____
_____

Food, Dining & Restaurants: _____
_____
_____
_____

Highlights / Memorable Events: _____
_____
_____
_____

Places To Go & Things To Do for Next Time: _____
_____
_____
_____

Notes:

Date: _____ From: _____ Beginning Mileage: _____

Weather: To: _____ Ending Mileage: _____

Route Taken: _____

_____ Total Miles Traveled: _____

Campground Information

Name: _____ Our Rating: ☆ ☆ ☆ ☆

Address: _____ GPS: _____

Phone: _____ Altitude: _____

Site # _____ $ _____ ☐ Day ☐ Week ☐ Month Cell Service / Carrier: _____

☐ First Visit	☐ Return Visit	☐ Easy Access	☐ Antenna Reception ☐ Satellite TV ☐ Cable TV
☐ Site Level	☐ Back-in	☐ Pull-through	☐ Wifi Available ☐ Free ☐ Fee $_____
☐ 15 amp	☐ 30 amp	☐ 50 amp	
☐ Water	☐ Sewer	☐ Shade ☐ Sun	Memberships: _____
☐ Paved	☐ Sand / Grass	☐ Gravel	Amenities: _____
☐ Picnic Table	☐ Fire ring	☐ Trees ☐ Lawn	Location ☺ 😐 ☹ Water Pressure ☺ 😐 ☹
☐ Patio	☐ Kid Friendly	☐ Pet Friendly	Restrooms ☺ 😐 ☹ Laundry ☺ 😐 ☹
☐ Store	☐ Cafe	☐ Firewood	Pool ☺ 😐 ☹ Hot Tub ☺ 😐 ☹
☐ Ice	☐ Secuiryt	☐ Quiet ☐ Noisy	

Places Visited / Activities: _____

_____

_____

_____

People Met / New Friends: _____

_____

_____

_____

Food, Dining & Restaurants: _____

_____

_____

_____

Highlights / Memorable Events: _____

_____

_____

_____

Places To Go & Things To Do for Next Time: _____

_____

_____

_____

Notes:

Made in the USA
San Bernardino, CA
31 January 2019